CHAKRA HEALING

CHAKRA HEALING

A Beginner's Guide to Self-Healing Techniques That Balance the Chakras

Margarita Alcantara

FALL RIVER PRESS

New York

I dedicate this book to my grandmother,
Lola Anunciacion Pineda Perlas,
who always believed in me.

FALL RIVER PRESS

New York

An Imprint of Sterling Publishing Co., Inc.
1166 Avenue of the Americas
New York, NY 10036

This publication is intended for informational purposes only. The publisher does not claim that this
publication shall provide or guarantee any benefits, healing, cure, or any results in any respect. This
publication is not intended to provide or replace conventional medical advice, treatment, or diagnosis
or be a substitute to consulting with a physician or other licensed medical or health-care providers.
The publisher shall not be liable or responsible in any respect for any use or application of any content
contained in this publication or any adverse effects, consequence, loss, or damage of any type resulting
or arising from, directly or indirectly, the use or application of any content contained in this
publication. Any trademarks are the property of their respective owners, are used for editorial
purposes only, and the publisher makes no claim of ownership and shall acquire no right, title,
or interest in such trademarks by virtue of this publication.

ISBN 978-1-4351-6753-7

For information about custom editions, special sales, and premium and
corporate purchases, please contact Sterling Special Sales at 800-805-5489
or specialsales@sterlingpublishing.com.

Manufactured in the United States of America
4 6 8 10 9 7 5 3

sterlingpublishing.com

A LOOK AHEAD

● ● ● ● ● ● ● ●

Chakra healing is a powerful art that can improve your life in every way—I'm excited to share my love of chakras with you so you can learn to heal yourself from within.

In Part 1, I'll introduce the concept of chakras so you can get a good foundation on your energy centers. This is a great place to begin if you're new to chakras and need an entry-level overview.

If you're ready to dive into more detailed methodologies for each chakra, flip ahead to page 22, where the different chakra charts begin. If you're curious to learn about the various ways in which people work with chakras—from meditation to yoga to crystal healing—browse the "Harnessing Your Chakra Power" section starting on page 37.

Whether you know it or not, your chakras are an important driving factor in every aspect of your daily life. Part 2 addresses common imbalances that manifest on physical, mental, emotional, and spiritual levels, and it offers helpful techniques to begin healing these imbalances, one chakra at a time.

To learn more about which of your chakras may need balancing, turn to page 54 and look for the symptoms or ailments with which you may be struggling.

Once you've identified which chakra or chakras you'd like to balance or heal, begin working through the chakra healing techniques that start on page 55.

I hope you find that the lessons in this book bring you closer to living the life you want to lead. Happy reading—and happy healing!

CONTENTS

• • • • • • •

Introduction 8

Ⅰ THE POWERFUL CHAKRA SYSTEM 10

1 An Overview of the Chakras 12

2 Working with the Chakras 36

Ⅱ HEALING YOUR CHAKRAS 52

3 Common Symptoms and Ailments 54

4 Healing Remedies and Treatments 85

Appendix A: Yoga Poses 146

Appendix B: Crystals 158

Resources 175

References 176

Index 177

Acknowledgments 189

About the Author 190

INTRODUCTION

● ● ● ● ● ● ● ●

When my new patient, Ms. B, first walked into my office, I could feel her disappointment with where she was in life. Whenever a new patient walks through my door, I "listen" to what their chakras have to say.

Ms. B's initial appointment was acupuncture treatment for stress and ankle pain. As a licensed acupuncturist, I use Traditional Chinese Medicine. I began by feeling her pulse and reading her tongue to assess the health of her organs. But, as with most patients, something deeper than physical issues brought Ms. B to my door. I knew there was more that Ms. B wanted to address than ankle pain and stress from her job—even if she didn't yet realize it herself.

I grew up as an empath. Though you might have first heard this term—rooted in the word *empathy*—it is used to refer to someone who intuitively feels what others are feeling, almost as if they were feeling it themselves. Like many others, I didn't immediately understand what an empath was or how to embrace my intuitive gifts. I was often dismissed by others as being overly sensitive or awkward. So, in an effort to fit in, I disconnected from that part of myself. Clearly, this sensitivity thing was causing me problems! But when we shut ourselves off from who we really are, our bodies often become "talkative" through physical, emotional, mental, and/or spiritual symptoms—until we pay attention to them and rectify the situation.

As Ms. B and I discussed her medical health and the symptoms she was seeking treatment for, I sensed she was carrying fear. Not coincidentally, she soon told me that she felt creatively stifled at her job, which she hated. She really wanted to be a yoga instructor and write about healing and holistic wellness, but she was scared to strike out on her own. She didn't trust her inner wisdom, and was moving through life identifying with past pains—pains that were holding her back from these goals.

Through acupuncture, Reiki, crystal work, and lots of compassion, Ms. B soon blossomed, balancing the emotions she hadn't been allowing herself to feel (which were keeping her from feeling joy), and honoring the ways she wanted to creatively express herself. She quit the job she hated, completed her yoga training, and started writing for a wellness website. And by the end of our treatments, her ankle pain had resolved. After a while, she was only coming in for maintenance care.

Like Ms. B, we all create stories for ourselves—stories that inform how we live our lives. While some of these stories may be true, most are usually outdated. Oftentimes, we carry the pain from these false stories in our bodies. More specifically, we carry them in our energy centers, otherwise known as *chakras*. By learning what we each carry in our individual energy systems, we can empower ourselves on deep levels to transform into the radiant creatures we were meant to be. And that is the purpose of this book—to familiarize you with what you're carrying in your chakras, so you can heal yourself from within.

Whether you're new to the world of chakras and energy healing and need a foundational primer to get you started, or you already have a deep knowledge of the system and want a refresher on the basics, this book will help you heal yourself, through understanding and care of your chakras.

I

THE POWERFUL CHAKRA SYSTEM

In Part 1, you will build your foundation of knowledge about the chakra system. Chapter 1 introduces you to the unique qualities and powers of the seven major energy centers in your body, so you can better understand why it's important to keep them balanced and free of blockages. In Chapter 2 you'll learn about the different healing techniques that have been developed to keep the chakra system healthy. Learning about these different techniques may help you figure out which healing method suits you best.

1

AN OVERVIEW OF THE CHAKRAS

• • • • • • •

In this chapter, I'll introduce the chakra system—
what chakras are, how to feel them, how they work,
some myths and warnings about chakra healing
work, and how to safely engage with your energy
centers. You'll learn about each chakra's individual
characteristics and the possible causes for energy
blocks, as well as what happens to your physical,
emotional, mental, and spiritual health when your
chakras are in—or out—of harmony.

What Are Chakras?

You are already familiar with your physical body. You know how it feels to flex or extend an area of your body; that your muscles are attached to your bones; that your nerves signal to your limbs, torso, and head; and that what you eat and drink affects your health. In these ways, you can already see how aspects of your physical being are connected to each other, and how your perceptions through touch, smell, taste, sight, and hearing inform each other, creating your life experiences.

However, your physical body is not the only body you have. Whether you're studying chakras or quantum physics, you come to learn that everything is energy, with its own vibrational frequency. From the most basic atoms that create our cells, organs, bones, muscles, and bodily systems to the most expansive planet in the solar system, everything is made up of energy. And that energy has many names: qi, ki, chi, prana, mana, Odic force, bioplasm, and life force energy, among many others.

The energy body is the human energy field that extends beyond the physical body. Much as your physical body consists of many layers—your nervous system, musculature, and skeletal system— with intricate, overlapping functions, your energy body also consists of many interacting layers. Like your physical body, each layer serves a specific purpose and the layers work collectively as one. Together, the layers of your energy body are called your aura. Your aura interacts with your physical body as well as your energy centers, or chakras.

The word *chakra* is derived from the Sanskrit word *cakra*, meaning "wheel." It was first mentioned in the Vedas, ancient Hindu texts that date to around 1,500 BCE. Throughout history, many cultures—including the Egyptians, Hindus, Chinese, Sufis,

Zarathustrians, Greeks, Native Americans, Incas, and the Maya, among others—have all known these energy centers, or the chakra system, to be a reflection of the natural law that exists within the universe and an intertwined counterpart to our physical selves.

Chakras are energy vortexes that exist within each of us. These energy vortexes transport energy from the universe around you into your aura and body, as well as between the physical body and the layers of your aura. You can think of your chakra system as similar to a spiritual bloodstream. Blood carries oxygen, nutrients, and hormones throughout the body; helps regulate and balance the body; and protects the body by removing waste products and clotting when the body is harmed. Much in the same way your bloodstream connects and supports your many other physical bodily systems, your chakra system connects and supports your physical self and your energy self.

All living things—humans, animals, plants, trees, even the Earth—have a chakra system, a living system of energy vortexes, that exists within them. There are seven major chakras in the body, as well as several minor ones. Each one is associated with specific organs and glands, physical functions and dysfunctions, and emotional, mental, and spiritual issues. We'll get into more specifics about each later in this chapter.

When we get in touch with the energy within our chakras, we connect with ourselves more fully, and learn how to heal ourselves on all levels, creating true holistic healing. This is why mindfulness-based practices, such as meditation, help connect the mind with body and spirit, why certain physical activities can help clear your head and feel more centered, and why cultivating your spirit heals your mind and body.

It is all connected.

FEEL YOUR CHAKRAS

• • • • • • •

To get in touch with your energy, hold your hands one inch apart, palms facing each other. Get familiar with the warmth and energy exchange between your hands (our hands contain minor chakras). Separate your hands slightly, "stretching out" the energy between your palms. Then bring them closer together again, condensing your energy. Repeat a few times, playing with the energy between the palms of your hands. Don't worry if you don't seem to feel anything at first. Relax, clear your mind, and continue the practice, remaining open and in tune with yourself.

As you become more familiar with your energy, you will not only be able to notice the warmth of your hands (which will increase, even when your hands are farther apart), but also a slight energy charge between them. With time and patience, you'll be able to feel this charge more strongly, even when you separate your hands farther apart.

You can feel your major chakras, too. For instance, to feel your heart chakra, place both hands at the center of your chest. Take a slow steady breath through your nose. Feel the warmth and inner glow underneath your hands. You are not only feeling your heartbeat, or the coursing of your blood, but also the sensation of your heart chakra expanding.

Feel it? Congratulations, you are now getting in touch with your chakras! If you don't feel anything yet, don't worry. With time and practice, your sensitivity will increase.

The Power of Chakras to Heal

Knowledge of chakras for healing and enlightenment is ancient wisdom—wisdom that has been known in many ancient cultures for centuries. More recent interest in chakras is because we are starting to feel, more and more, that focusing solely on our physical health is not bringing us complete wellness. Despite the many breakthroughs of modern medicine, something still feels missing or "off," even though we can't quite put our finger on it.

As the daughter of a Western physician, I am fully aware of Western medicine's contributions to health, and appreciate its value. I grew up reading my father's medical references, and learned that the human body is pretty amazing. Even so, I believe people collectively are starting to realize that somehow—even if we don't understand it—other factors may influence our current health challenges.

What if you learned that many of the physical symptoms we experience (barring events like car accidents and other direct physical trauma) could be prevented, simply because many of our physical symptoms are expressions of what hasn't been addressed in the energy body?

Enter the chakras.

When our chakras are in balance, our lives are in complete harmony and our health is good. If a chakra becomes blocked, we will eventually experience emotional distress or disease.

Because everything is energy, when we heal and maintain our energy body's health—through modalities like acupuncture, Reiki, meditation, yoga, and qi gong, among others—and make better lifestyle and diet choices, we actually heal issues that may come up *before* they manifest in the physical body.

MYTHS ABOUT CHAKRA HEALING

Before we get into the specifics of the chakra system, I want to dispel some myths about chakra healing work.

Myth 1: Chakra healing is an outside job. Whether or not you receive outside healing assistance from a practitioner in your chakra healing journey, in the end, *you* are the one who is the healer of you, not someone else. This is something I always tell my patients. Even though I may sometimes use the term "healer" in connection with what I do, healing is *always* an inside job. While healing practitioners can guide you on your journey, we are each responsible for our own healing.

Myth 2: Chakra healing is affiliated with a specific religion. Although the original sources of the chakra system came from religious texts, chakra healing has since expanded to reach a broader understanding and practice, and is now embraced by people from many walks of life. Cultivating chakra health has become an important practice for many on a spiritual path, and is not associated with religion.

Myth 3: Chakra healing is a form of demonic, or dark, ritual. True chakra healing, done right, is quite the opposite of demonic. You are infusing light, awareness, and consciousness into your body, mind, spirit, and heart—all of which dispel darkness.

CHAKRA HEALING WARNINGS

When engaging with healing your chakras, there are a few things you should remember as you begin.

Be patient with yourself. I often find that those who are just starting to get in touch with their chakras lose patience with themselves very quickly. Often, they begin to judge themselves as failures if they don't see immediate progress. Please remember that everyone is different, everyone has their own perfect timeline of their personal unfolding, and everything is happening exactly as it should, including your healing. Chakra healing, whether it is being cultivated to address a specific issue or to attain enlightenment, is an inner exploration, not a goal. Because of this, just as with physical healing, chakra healing is not something you can simply "speed up." However, receiving healing treatments and other techniques can clear out energetic debris and bring your energy centers more into harmony. Transformation takes patience. Be compassionate with yourself as you bloom.

Do not push yourself past what is comfortable, or force your energy. When people are eager to connect with their chakras, they often push themselves past what is comfortable. However, you may soon find yourself with a headache (literally!). As soon as you start feeling some resistance, take a break.

Get help from a healing practitioner when it's necessary. You can accomplish a lot on your own, but sometimes guidance can be helpful, especially if you feel like you're hitting a wall in your healing journey, or the pain manifested is affecting your quality of life. If and when you decide to get help, make sure the practitioner is licensed or certified in their modality. Check them out thoroughly before making an appointment. Ensure it'll be a good fit for you, and that you will feel safe.

Chakra Basics

The foundation of the chakra system consists of seven major chakras within the body. They each serve a purpose and are all interconnected.

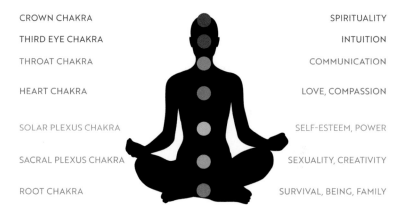

CROWN CHAKRA	SPIRITUALITY
THIRD EYE CHAKRA	INTUITION
THROAT CHAKRA	COMMUNICATION
HEART CHAKRA	LOVE, COMPASSION
SOLAR PLEXUS CHAKRA	SELF-ESTEEM, POWER
SACRAL PLEXUS CHAKRA	SEXUALITY, CREATIVITY
ROOT CHAKRA	SURVIVAL, BEING, FAMILY

The upper three are considered the spiritual chakras. The spiritual chakras focus on our connection to the Divine, as well as our Higher Self—that version of ourself that is tapped into our purest expression of love, wisdom, and power. The lower three chakras are considered the physical chakras. They ground us as human beings on Earth. Both the spiritual and physical chakras are connected in the center through the heart chakra.

ACTIVATING YOUR KUNDALINI ENERGY

• • • • • • •

Kundalini energy is the primal, enlightening force that awakens all of your chakras, often around the same time. We all have this energy, but it's usually dormant, lying quietly and coiled (like a snake) at the base of the spine, or root chakra.

You may have heard that working with chakras can awaken this Kundalini energy, and it's true—starting to open one's chakras does give a possibility of that happening. However, it's unlikely that the Kundalini would awaken suddenly, after reading a book or trying a few chakra healing techniques. The process typically occurs over a period of time, and it usually happens with people who have been actively and regularly cultivating it in their lives, perhaps by practicing Kundalini yoga or by regularly receiving or performing energy work.

When done safely, gradually, with supervision, and while cultivating your spirit, awakening your Kundalini energy can be full of joy, profound consciousness, and heightened psychic and intuitive sensibilities. For this reason, those who seek enlightenment often try to activate it through various practices, including Kundalini yoga and meditation.

However, if the Kundalini energy awakens spontaneously, through yoga or otherwise (such as interacting with someone, like a guru, whose Kundalini has already been awakened), and you aren't fully prepared for it or have blocks in your chakras, the energy can get stuck. It can be very difficult to manage the painful physical symptoms brought on by the massive energy shooting throughout your body. In some cases, these intense energy surges can lead the unprepared initiate to mental and emotional instability. When your Kundalini energy has been spontaneously awakened, and you're not prepared for it, finding a good spiritual teacher to help you move through it is crucial.

In addition, activating your Kundalini is not the only way to summon your chakra power. Indeed, arousing Kundalini energy has stood the test of time. However, other paths to awakening your chakras are more gentle and pleasant.

THE ROOT CHAKRA

The first of the physical chakras is the root chakra—the chakra largely responsible for how safe and secure you feel.

When the Root Chakra Is Out of Harmony

When the root chakra is out of harmony, there is an inability to trust nature. We also feel ungrounded, feel disconnected from Mother Earth, have issues around tribal beliefs (our identity in relationship to tribal consciousness) or family wounds, do not feel secure in the knowledge that our most basic and primal needs are being met (such as food, shelter, clothing, and love), function out of fear, and feel unsafe.

When the Root Chakra Is In Harmony

When the root chakra is in harmony, we are profoundly connected to nature, feel grounded, trust in the natural laws, and are able to move with the ebb and flow of life. We also come from a place of understanding that we will always be provided for, that we are connected to our tribal consciousness and family in healthy ways, and we feel safe.

SANSKRIT NAME
Muladhara

OTHER NAMES
First chakra, base chakra

LOCATION
At the perineum, between
the genitals and the anus,
base of spine

COLOR
Red

ELEMENT
Earth

AFFIRMATION
"I am"

GLANDS
Adrenals

PHYSICAL BODY PARTS
The physical body, base of spine,
legs, bones, feet, rectum, immune
system, large intestine, teeth

LIFE LESSON
To feel safe and secure in the
"physical plane," to manifest
our basic needs, and to cultivate
healthy (physical) sexuality

PHYSICAL DYSFUNCTION
Chronic lower back pain, sciatica,
varicose veins, rectal tumors/
cancer, hemorrhoids, constipation,
degenerative arthritis, knee
problems, depression, immune-
related disorders, weight problems

MENTAL/EMOTIONAL ISSUES
Physical family and group safety
and security, ability to provide for
life's necessities, ability to stand
up for self

**POSSIBLE CAUSES OF
ENERGY BLOCKS**
Fear of being alive, guilt

CRYSTALS
Ruby, garnet, black tourmaline,
bloodstone, hematite, obsidian,
onyx, red jasper, lodestone,
smoky quartz, fire agate

ESSENTIAL OILS
Myrrh, vetiver, sandalwood,
patchouli, spikenard

THE SACRAL PLEXUS CHAKRA

Located above the root chakra is the sacral plexus chakra—the second chakra, and the one most closely connected with sexual and reproductive activities, as well as emotions and creativity.

When the Sacral Plexus Chakra Is Out of Harmony

We have difficulty expressing our feelings (or are cut off from them), are out of touch with pleasure, and hold unprocessed anger. We feel stifled in our creativity and resentful for not being able to birth our ideas into the world. We also may have relationship issues (platonic and romantic), reproductive issues, or feel unstable or unhealthy around aspects of our sexuality. There will also be feelings of shame. We also may have issues around money and abundance, either placing an overemphasis on obtaining material goods, or not owning our abundance at all.

When the Sacral Plexus Chakra Is In Harmony

We are in the flow of our creative expression, in touch with pleasure, able to share (and express) feelings in healthy ways, create and maintain healthy relationships, and are connected to the emotional aspects of sexuality in ways that sustain us. We feel at peace with our abundance, and may even be in touch with our clairsentience (the gift of taking in intuitive information through feeling). We also have a healthy relationship to money, and easily cultivate abundance in our lives in balanced ways.

SANSKRIT NAME
Svadisthana

OTHER NAMES
Second chakra, sacral chakra, pelvic chakra, naval chakra

LOCATION
Two inches below the navel

COLOR
Orange

ELEMENT
Water

AFFIRMATION
"I feel"

GLANDS
Ovaries, testicles

PHYSICAL BODY PARTS
Womb, genitals, lower vertebrae, pelvis, appendix, bladder, hip area, kidneys

LIFE LESSON
To use emotions to connect with others without losing our identity, and to freely express creativity and healthy (emotional) sexuality

PHYSICAL DYSFUNCTION
Chronic lower back pain, sciatica, gynecological problems, pelvic pain, impotence, frigidity, uterine/bladder/kidney problems

MENTAL/EMOTIONAL ISSUES
Guilt and blame, money, sex, power and control, creativity, ethics, honor in relationships

POSSIBLE CAUSES OF ENERGY BLOCKS
Sexual abuse or trauma, rape, gender issues

CRYSTALS
Carnelian, amber, moonstone, coral, orange tourmaline, sunstone

ESSENTIAL OILS
Ylang ylang, lemon, patchouli, rosewood, sandalwood

THE SOLAR PLEXUS CHAKRA

Above the sacral plexus chakra is the chakra that corresponds with our personality, self-esteem, and sense of worth—the solar plexus chakra.

When the Solar Plexus Chakra Is Out of Harmony

We have a need to dominate and control, have a great need for prestige and keeping up appearances, and we function through the world with deep feelings of inadequacy. In short, we do not respect ourselves, and may even manifest self-hatred. We may give away our power to others, leaving us with no sense of self.

When the Solar Plexus Chakra Is In Harmony

We feel whole, centered in who we are, know our self-worth, cultivate our personal power in healthy ways, and are in touch with our inner warrior. There is a balance between spiritual and material worlds, we develop tolerance and acceptance (of ourselves and others), and feel inner peace and calm.

SANSKRIT NAME
Manipura

OTHER NAMES
Third chakra, power chakra

LOCATION
Two inches above the navel

COLOR
Yellow

ELEMENT
Fire

AFFIRMATION
"I can"

GLANDS
Pancreas, adrenals

PHYSICAL BODY PARTS
Abdomen, stomach, upper intestines, liver, gallbladder, spleen, middle spine

LIFE LESSON
To experience the depth of who we are with self-empowerment and self-esteem, to live our life task or soul's life purpose

PHYSICAL DYSFUNCTION
Arthritis, gastric or duodenal ulcers, colon/intestinal problems, pancreatitis/diabetes, chronic or acute indigestion, anorexia or bulimia, liver or adrenal dysfunction, fatigue, hepatitis, diabetes

MENTAL/EMOTIONAL ISSUES
Trust, fear, intimidation, self-esteem, self-confidence, self-respect, care of self and others, responsibility for making decisions, sensitivity to criticism, personal honor

POSSIBLE CAUSES OF ENERGY BLOCKS
Stuffed or repressed anger, issues of control especially in areas related to power

CRYSTALS
Yellow citrine, amber, yellow topaz, yellow tiger's eye, yellow agate, rutilated quartz

ESSENTIAL OILS
Lemon, lavender, rosewood, Roman chamomile, rosemary

THE HEART CHAKRA

The heart chakra holds our connection to both the physical and the spiritual aspects of ourselves. Because it is at this pivotal location—connecting the physical and spiritual chakras—it is also how we get in touch with our Higher Self in relation to the rest of the world (and even the universe).

When the Heart Chakra Is Out of Harmony

We are disconnected from ourselves, have difficulty loving ourselves or giving love from a genuine place, do not feel deserving of love (and therefore have difficulty receiving love), are out of touch with who we are, and develop depression (from lack of connection to self).

When the Heart Chakra Is In Harmony

We are fully connected to ourselves, cultivate joy easily, love and accept ourselves (and, as an extension, others). We give and receive love genuinely, and cultivate compassion for self and others.

SANSKRIT NAME
Anahata

OTHER NAMES
Fourth chakra

LOCATION
At the center of the chest

COLOR
Green

ELEMENT
Air

AFFIRMATION
"I love"

GLANDS
Thymus

PHYSICAL BODY PARTS
Heart, pericardium, circulatory system, lungs, shoulders, arms, ribs, breasts, diaphragm

LIFE LESSON
To experience compassion and connection with oneself and others

PHYSICAL DYSFUNCTION
Congestive heart failure, heart attack, heart disease, asthma/allergies, lung cancer, bronchial pneumonia, lung disease, breast cancer, high blood pressure

MENTAL/EMOTIONAL ISSUES
Love and hatred, resentment, grief, self-centeredness, loneliness, forgiveness, compassion, hope, trust

POSSIBLE CAUSES OF ENERGY BLOCKS
Repressed heartache or grief

CRYSTALS
Rose quartz, emerald, green tourmaline, jade, green calcite, green kyanite, peridot

ESSENTIAL OILS
Rose, geranium, neroli, palmarosa, bergamot, lavender, melissa/lemon balm, ylang ylang

THE THROAT CHAKRA

The first of the spiritual chakras—the throat chakra—has much to do with our true, authentic voice, where faith and understanding combine.

When the Throat Chakra Is Out of Harmony

We have difficulty speaking our truth or expressing ourselves, feel silenced and judged for what we say, feel out of alignment with who we are, and feel out of touch with our will to live.

When the Throat Chakra Is In Harmony

Our will to live is strong and we are able to follow our dreams. We speak our truth—where we say what we mean and mean what we say. We express ourselves easily, creatively, and authentically, listen to our inner voice, and have a balance between silence and speech.

SANSKRIT NAME
Vishuddha

OTHER NAMES
Fifth chakra

LOCATION
At the front of the base of
the neck, at the hollow
of the collarbone

COLOR
Light blue

ELEMENT
Sound

AFFIRMATION
"I speak"

GLANDS
Thyroid, parathyroid

PHYSICAL BODY PARTS
Throat, trachea, neck vertebrae,
mouth, teeth and gums,
esophagus, hypothalamus,
shoulders, arms, hands

LIFE LESSON
To speak and receive the Truth

PHYSICAL DYSFUNCTION
Raspy or sore throat, mouth
ulcers, gum difficulties, TMJ, stiff
neck, scoliosis, swollen glands,
thyroid problems

MENTAL/EMOTIONAL ISSUES
Strength of will, personal
expression, following one's dream,
using personal power to create,
choice and capacity to make
decisions, addiction, judgment,
criticism, faith

**POSSIBLE CAUSES OF
ENERGY BLOCKS**
Difficulty in expressing oneself,
withholding or swallowing words,
suppressing creative talents

CRYSTALS
Turquoise, blue kyanite,
aquamarine, celestite, iolite,
sodalite, lapis lazuli

ESSENTIAL OILS
Lavender, rosemary, frankincense,
German chamomile, hyssop

THE THIRD EYE CHAKRA

The sixth chakra—the third eye chakra—is associated with our "sixth sense"; it is the center of our wisdom, spiritual insight, and intuition.

When the Third Eye Chakra Is Out of Harmony

We focus only on our intellect and reject all spiritual aspects of ourselves. We do not trust (nor are aware of) our intuition, are only able to see the physical reality in life, and carry a lot of fear in regard to our inner wisdom.

When the Third Eye Chakra Is In Harmony

We invite our intuition and awareness into everyday aspects of life. We trust our inner vision and act upon what our intuition tells us (which makes it stronger). We have a deep knowing beyond what we can physically see, and are even in touch with our clairvoyance (the gift of taking in intuitive information through sight and vision).

SANSKRIT NAME
Ajna

OTHER NAMES
Sixth chakra, brow chakra, forehead chakra

LOCATION
Between the eyebrows

COLOR
Indigo

ELEMENT
Light

AFFIRMATION
"I see"

GLANDS
Pineal

PHYSICAL BODY PARTS
Brain, nervous system, eyes, ears, nose

LIFE LESSON
To use insight and intuition, to see past the physical

PHYSICAL DYSFUNCTION
Brain tumor/hemorrhage, stroke, neurological disturbances, blindness, deafness, full spinal difficulties, learning disabilities, seizures, headaches, blurred vision

MENTAL/EMOTIONAL ISSUES
Self-evaluation, truth, intellectual abilities, feelings of adequacy, openness to the ideas of others, ability to learn from experience, emotional intelligence

POSSIBLE CAUSES OF ENERGY BLOCKS
A lack of trust in one's intuition

CRYSTALS
Lapis lazuli, amethyst, fluorite, lepidolite, sugilite, tanzanite, clear quartz, star sapphire, kyanite

ESSENTIAL OILS
Lavender, frankincense, sandalwood

THE CROWN CHAKRA

The last of the spiritual chakras—the crown chakra—is a source of connection to the Divine and our higher selves.

When the Crown Chakra Is Out of Harmony

We feel totally disconnected from the Divine/Source/Universe/God/dess. We may even have anger at God. We have difficulty trusting our path, and our lives in general. We feel depressed, alone, unsatisfied with life, and unable to let go of anxiety and fear.

When the Crown Chakra Is In Harmony

We live in the knowledge of Unity—the idea that we are all connected. We understand that we are individual reflections of the Divine, trust that we are connected to the Divine, and understand that our individual identity goes beyond the physical form. We are also more able to easily elevate our consciousness.

SANSKRIT NAME
Sahasrara

OTHER NAMES
Seventh chakra

LOCATION
At the top and center of the head

COLOR
Purple, white, gold

ELEMENT
Thought

AFFIRMATION
"I know"

GLANDS
Pituitary

PHYSICAL BODY PARTS
Muscular system, skeletal system, skin, cerebral cortex, central nervous system

LIFE LESSON
To experience the divine meaning of life

PHYSICAL DYSFUNCTION
Energetic disorders, depression, chronic exhaustion that is not linked to physical disorder, extreme sensitivity to light/sound/other environmental factors, confusion, apathy, alienation

MENTAL/EMOTIONAL ISSUES
Ability to trust life, values, ethics, courage, selflessness, ability to see the larger pattern or picture, faith, inspiration, spirituality, devotion

POSSIBLE CAUSES OF ENERGY BLOCKS
Lack of trust in the Divine or life, unresolved anger toward the Divine

CRYSTALS
Amethyst, clear quartz, Herkimer diamond, labradorite, moonstone, selenite, phenacite, kunzite, apophyllite, white topaz

ESSENTIAL OILS
Frankincense, peppermint, sandalwood, lotus

2

WORKING WITH
THE CHAKRAS

• • • • • •

In this chapter, we'll discuss the most common methods used by practitioners to harness chakra power, how these methods work, and also share recommendations for when to receive a professional acupuncture or Reiki treatment to help heal the chakras. I'll also offer advice on how to maintain a balanced chakra system and create a sacred healing space at home or in your office.

Harnessing Your Chakra Power

There are a number of different methods we can use at home to help heal our chakras, including visualizations and meditations, changing old habits, practicing yoga, using crystals and essential oils, and getting the most out of our food. Because different people feel drawn to different healing techniques, a range of methods are covered in this book. I generally recommend that my patients choose healing techniques that they feel most drawn to, since one technique is not necessarily better than the other.

That being said, if you're experiencing physical problems, it may help to begin with dietary changes, yoga, massage, acupuncture, and other bodywork first. If your struggles relate to the mind or heart, meditation, crystal work, or essential oils might be a good starting point.

MEDITATION AND VISUALIZATIONS

Meditation is a form of mental exercise that trains the mind to stay focused on a particular object, goal, or sensation, such as your breath.

Purpose

Meditation is a way to calm mental chatter. When practiced regularly, it can help transform consciousness in a way that promotes inner peace, mental clarity, emotional positivity, deep knowing, and concentration, as well as ground us when we feel scattered. By maintaining a specific focus, like the breath, a mantra, or another tool, the mind can stop wandering and getting lost in thoughts, emotions, or other mental distractions. Meditations can also include visualizations, where you create a mental image toward a specific purpose. Envisioning the colors or flow within a chakra can help you connect to them and strengthen them.

Because meditation involves the ability to observe distracting thoughts and emotions without judgment, we learn to control our reactions to stimuli that might otherwise create painful or upsetting reactions. This skill—called mindfulness—can be an incredibly powerful tool for cultivating calm and compassion in your daily life. For the purposes of this book, it can also be a way of connecting with, and strengthening, your chakras. You can use meditation to get in touch with what you're holding in a particular energy center, helping you become more connected with your physical and energy bodies.

How It's Implemented

There are many ways to meditate—you can be sitting or lying down, you can be still or meditate while engaging in an activity such as walking, creating art, playing music, or journaling. Some people practice 5 to 10 minutes a day, while others may meditate for longer. In part 2 of this book, we'll cover different meditation exercises that help heal the different chakras. Most will not require you to meditate for longer than 5 to 10 minutes at a time.

Why/How It Works

Meditation is a practice that has been time-tested throughout the ages. It has enjoyed a resurgence of interest in the past couple of years, no doubt because many of us want to cultivate a practice to quiet our mind and create peace within our busy lifestyles! But it's not just a fad. In fact, one 2016 study in *Consciousness and Cognition* found that just a single session of meditation reduces physiological symptoms of anger—in seasoned and novice meditators alike.

Pros/Cons of Using This Method

Pros: On the positive side, meditation can be done anytime, anywhere, within any time frame. It creates a deeper connection with the self and makes it easier for us to shift into higher consciousness. It also helps us access our capacity to self-heal and create mindfulness, which then extends peace into the rest of our lives. Also, because this practice builds upon itself, meditation helps with any self-study practice you may already have.

Cons: Two words: "monkey mind." Your mind will want to distract you from your practice, typically by calling up tasks for the day, like what you will be having for dinner, or thoughts you have been avoiding, like worrying about your savings. Even seasoned practitioners of meditation experience monkey mind. Meditation is called a "practice" for a reason: cultivating a sense of deep awareness and inner peace using meditation takes time. It is not an overnight quick fix.

CHANGING OLD HABITS

Breaking old bad habits can help you heal imbalances in your chakras by creating new, healthier habits.

Purpose

Behavioral and lifestyle changes help us interrupt our regular everyday patterns of thinking and reacting to the environment. Oftentimes, imbalances that we hold in our chakras can be healed, in part, by shifting our consciousness around long-standing beliefs about ourselves and how we interact with others.

How It's Implemented

The first step to breaking old habits is creating awareness around the bad habit, as well as creating awareness around an issue that we are holding in a specific chakra. Once we're aware of a problem behavior or bad habit, we can then work to change that behavior, or respond differently.

For example, consider when you don't speak up for yourself in a romantic relationship. Not expressing your needs and wants can be an indication that your throat chakra is not balanced. To interrupt this pattern, you might make a mental note whenever you notice yourself shutting down after a heated discussion. Once you're aware you are silencing yourself, stop and ask how you could react differently. Then, apply the new reaction. Any new reaction will meet this goal though productive, healthy reactions will be more helpful than unhealthy or rash ones. Perhaps you choose to connect with your partner, in a way that they can hear you, about how the heated discussion made you feel. In this way, you help heal the silencing pattern in your throat chakra. We also change the story of identifying as "someone who keeps their mouth shut" to "someone who is working to communicate effectively."

Shifting consciousness around an old pattern takes practice and patience. However, doing it long enough allows us to break old habits that no longer serve us and create healthier ones.

Why/How It Works

This works because by modifying our approach to a recurring problem, we are actively engaged with changing old patterns that no longer work. When practiced long enough, and with consistency, we clear old patterns and beliefs held in specific chakras.

Pros/Cons of Using This Method

Pros: It works! Embracing new habits and using them to replace negative old habits brings positive, healthy results, even if you have yet to fully connect with your chakra system.

Cons: It can take time and a lot of repetition (and patience) before the new patterns stick.

YOGA

While there are many forms of yoga, the one most commonly practiced focuses on *asana*, the series of physical postures and breathing exercises aimed at strengthening us physically, mentally, and spiritually.

Purpose

Asana is the program of physical postures that provide physical strength and stamina and are designed to create awareness and connection with the body through movement. Asana yoga is a great tool for self-transformation on various levels—physical, mental, and spiritual.

How It's Implemented

Through physical exercises and breath, we connect the mind with the tissues of our body. A variety of yoga postures help open various locations within the body, which brings awareness and balance to the chakras. When practicing yoga asanas, we move the body into different physical postures and then hold those poses for set periods of time. At the same time, we control our breathing in different ways, helping energy circulate throughout the body and cultivating mindfulness. There are different yoga styles, some of which can be particularly useful in balancing the chakras. Kundalini yoga, for example, uses specific physical poses, chanting, breathing techniques, and meditation to try to awaken the Kundalini energy that moves through our chakras.

More advanced yoga postures have a higher risk of injury (headstand and shoulderstand, for example, are not appropriate for beginners or anyone with a neck injury) and should be done with the support and guidance of a trained yoga teacher.

Why/How It Works

Yoga helps bring vital life force into the chakras, creating awareness and opening the chakras. In general, yoga assists with grounding us in our bodies through a sensory experience. This is especially useful for those of us who tend to spend too much time in our heads, engaged in mental activities, and less time rooted in the Earth's energy, or fully present in our phyical bodies. It also brings attention to how our postures affect how we move through the world.

For example, when we experience grief, we have a tendency to bring our shoulders forward, creating a concave movement with our bodies. In relation to our energy body, we do this to protect our heart chakra. However, if we keep this posture for a long time, it can create physical problems in the shoulders or upper back. Practicing yoga helps us become aware of the tightness in our shoulders and upper back, engage with it, and ultimately release it.

Pros/Cons of Using This Method

Pros: Because yoga requires a lot of physical movement, it can be an excellent form of exercise. Yoga classes tend to be held in quiet studios, so they can be relaxing and great for stress management. Because yoga cultivates awareness of the body, some people find it helps them practice healthier eating habits and other positive lifestyle changes. Also, yoga doesn't usually require a lot of expensive equipment.

Cons: Yoga classes can be expensive, and they may not fit into everyone's schedules. While there are many free yoga videos online, learning yoga as a beginner can be difficult because without a teacher to guide them, it can be tough to know whether or not one is practicing specific poses properly. Some new practitioners experience pain, especially headaches or muscle soreness, while their body adjusts to the postures, energy shifts, and physical exertion of yoga practice. It also takes time to obtain optimal results from yoga, and yoga must be done in conjunction with self-study and cultivation of stillness to truly support chakra healing.

CRYSTALS

Crystals are used to draw out or redirect energy, as well as to develop the strengths associated with a particular stone. They are also used to rebalance and heal.

Purpose

Working with crystals and stones helps us engage with the natural Earth energy to nourish our strengths and gifts. It also helps us release what no longer serves us, tap into our gifts, restore balance, heal, and elevate consciousness. Crystals can be used in many ways to address various challenges.

How It's Implemented

There are many ways to work with crystals. One common way is to keep a small crystal on your person, whether worn as a pendant, earrings, or bracelet or carried in your pocket. Carrying a crystal on your body keeps its energetic frequency resonating with you throughout the day. Another way to work with stones, especially when doing chakra healing, is to lie down in a comfortable spot, place chakra-specific crystals on their particular chakra, and allow yourself to meditate (or simply clear your mind) while the stones amplify what you're currently working on—whether it be to release something from a certain chakra, cultivate your gifts, break patterns, or work toward another goal. Another great way to use crystals is to hold them in your left (receiving) hand during meditation, so you can receive the beneficial healing vibrations of the crystal.

Why/How It Works

Recall our earlier discussion of how everything is energy, vibrating at its own particular frequency. Crystals, too, each have their own particular vibration and purpose. By choosing one to help you with a certain goal, or by allowing yourself to be drawn to one in particular, you align yourself with the vibration of that stone, as it works directly with your energy body (and often benefits the physical body, as well). For instance, rose quartz not only helps the heart chakra, but also helps reduce blood pressure. It's all related.

Pros/Cons of Using This Method

Pros: Crystals are aesthetically pleasing to look at, effective, easy to use, and versatile to work with. The effects of crystal healing can also be easily felt; you can literally feel the pulsing in your hand when holding a crystal that is perfect for what you're working on.

Cons: It may take some time to become familiar with how to work with crystals. Cost and finding the right crystals may also be challenging—but the Internet makes it easier to find the specific crystals you need at a good value.

ESSENTIAL OILS

Essential oil therapy is an ancient healing practice that involves using natural, often fragrant, compounds that exist in many types of plants for their curative properties.

Purpose

Since discovering the healing benefits of certain plants, herbs, and flowers, people found ways to include them in our lives—by adding them to meals, creating medicines with them, topically applying them to affected areas, and distilling their scent essence. While many people already know that essential oils smell fragrant and pleasant, each plant also has its own energetic resonance, allowing each one to treat both the subtle energy body and the physical body. For those of us who think too much, essential oil therapy is great because it bypasses our thought processes and vibrates with us on a primal level. It can help us shift from being in a place where emotions are overwhelming, to a place where we feel more able to take a breath and ease into our next steps. It is also useful in bodywork, helping to release tension in the muscles and treat specific types of pain.

How It's Implemented

To help the chakras heal, applying 5 to 6 drops of a particular essential oil to a certain chakra can ground, center, release, or open it. Mix a few drops of your selected essential oil in a carrier oil and apply the chosen oils with a cotton ball, or massage them into the chakra directly. When using essential oils on the body, be sure to dilute them in carrier oils—particularly those that are highly irritating to the skin when used alone. They're called carrier oils because they actually carry the essential oil for application. A good carrier oil to use is jojoba, which you can find at your local health food store. You can enhance the healing experience by combining a meditative practice right after application of the essential oils.

Why/How It Works

Essential oil uses go deeper than simply smelling good. They access our energy body and physical body, often connecting them together in synergy, and creating healing on various levels. They are particularly effective for chakra healing because they bring the energetics of the oil to the chakra, helping us connect with it. And, because the healing happens on a base level, it bypasses the brain, immediately accessing our internal healing.

Pros/Cons of Using This Method

Pros: The healing that essential oil therapy brings is quickly accessible. Quality oils are also easy to find, they can travel with you, and there are many ways to work with them (by applying them to the body, diffusing them in your living or work space, creating blends and elixirs, among others).

Cons: Because some essential oils may irritate the skin, they are not recommended for topical application on the body without a carrier oil. Also, ingesting oils is not recommended, because they can inflame the digestive tract, and some oils (depending on the manufacturer) are adulterated. In addition, although essential oil therapy is powerful, it should be used in conjunction with other modalities to cultivate inner healing to help you achieve chakra balance.

FOOD AND DIET

Food is not only a way to sustain your physical body, but a way to support your energy body as well—the foods you eat can help your chakras heal energetically.

Purpose

When it comes to chakra health, because your energy body is directly connected to your physical body, what you ingest matters. Even our water intake can affect your health. More conscious food choices can go a long way to healing your body and promoting higher vibration of your chakras.

How It's Implemented

Ideally, the body functions at its best when eating foods that support its systems. Foods can be inflammatory: Dairy and gluten, for instance, can be inflammatory to skin, digestion, and joint health, and sugar is inflammatory to various body parts and systems.

REIKI, ACUPUNCTURE, AND THE CHAKRAS

• • • • • • •

When it comes to working with a professional to rebalance the chakras, there are a few different modalities to consider. Here, we'll cover Reiki and acupuncture.

Reiki is an energy healing technique in which a practitioner acts to channel unlimited life force energy to a patient or client to support their physical, emotional, mental, and spiritual healing and evolution. The Reiki practitioner acts as a conduit, using a gentle placement of hands ("hands on" or "hands off") to help balance the chakras. Reiki should always be undertaken with a certified Reiki practitioner.

Acupuncture, another traditional technique, uses precise needle placement to alleviate physical, mental, and emotional symptoms. While there is no official consensus around whether or not you can heal the chakras with acupuncture (some argue it is not an energy healing modality), acupuncture does move chi, and there are acupuncture points on chakras. In that light, it may be possible for acupuncture to address chakra imbalances. Again, acupuncture should only be undertaken with a licensed practitioner.

Sugars can create a negative impact for many of us if they're a big part of a diet. On the other hand, removing highly processed ingredients, such as white flour and white sugar, from your diet is a simple shift that can improve your health in many ways. When you eat more clean foods—foods that are less processed, more sustainably harvested, seasonal, organic, locally sourced, and made with fewer additives and more whole ingredients—your physical body benefits. When your physical body benefits, your energy body benefits as well.

Why/How It Works

Eating clean foods supports your physical and energy body health. Creating awareness around which foods work and don't work for your body helps all your body's systems; for instance, by promoting cell growth, bone growth, muscle, organ, and gland health, and mental functions. By extension, this all benefits your energy body.

Pros/Cons of Using This Method

Pros: There are many choices and options to support your physical and energy bodies with food, and when you implement them, it can be healing to both your physical and energy bodies.

Cons: Eating healthy is much easier said than done. Clean, organic, sustainably grown food can be expensive, and it can be tempting to purchase convenient fast food rather than cook healthy food at home.

Maintaining Balance in Your Daily Life

As we start to open up into the power of our chakras, it is important to maintain our raised vibration—positive energy—in daily life. Why? Because when we are healing ourselves on various levels and clearing our chakras of denser energies, it is important to keep our energy and space clear and protected, as well as keep our vibration resonating at a higher frequency. This helps maintain chakra balance.

Regularly cultivate mindfulness and practice gratefulness. By regularly cultivating mindfulness, we keep ourselves in the present. When we ruminate and get depressed, we often dwell on the past. When we experience anxiety, we are worrying about the future. Staying in the present allows us to show up fully for ourselves. Practicing gratefulness also elevates vibration.

Maintain your energy through movement. Whether it be yoga, qi gong, or other physical activity, it is important to regularly maintain clarity of mind, body, and spirit.

Bless yourself with sacred white sage. Sacred white sage is an herb used by Native Americans for its powerful clearing properties. It clears negative energy from your body or living space. Clearing a living space or ourselves with sacred white sage is called smudging. To smudge a living space, light the tip of a bunch of sage with a match or lighter; allow the smoke to plume; and use your hand or a feather wand to waft the smoke to areas of the home, starting clockwise from the front door, blessing all items along the way, until you reach the front door once more. To smudge yourself, use your hands to direct the smoke toward your body, blessing all parts of your body, especially your chakras down your midline. As you do so, say aloud, "I bless my arms, I bless my throat chakra, I bless my chest," and so on. Make sure to tap the loose ashes into a heat-resistant container every so often as you go along.

Epsom salt baths. Highly sensitive people—those who pick up other people's energy very easily—should consider taking Epsom salt baths once a week or every other week. The same holds true for those who have physical aches and pains, especially muscular ones. Epsom salt contains magnesium, which is easily absorbed through the skin during a bath and helps soothe muscular and other physical pain, as well as manage stress. In addition, it helps clear auras, which is especially useful for those who tend to take work home, have a difficult commute, work in a toxic office, or deal regularly with difficult people. Epsom salt baths are very detoxifying for your system, and can even be used to ward off colds.

Your Sacred Healing Space

To create a sacred healing space, make an altar at home. Some recommended items include the following:

Sacred white sage bundle. As mentioned previously, sacred white sage is used to smudge yourself and a location. To smudge a living space, light the tip with a match or lighter, allow the smoke to plume, then waft the smoke to areas of the space to be smudged.

Palo Santo. Palo Santo, or "holy wood" in Spanish, comes from a tree that grows in Central and South America. It clears energy and strongly disperses negativity, especially evil spirits. Use it much the same as sacred white sage.

Feather wand. Whether it is a large single feather or a wand bundle of feathers, for the purpose of smudging, use the feather wand to direct smoke toward areas to be cleansed.

Heat-resistant container. Use this to gather the ashes that may fall from burning sacred white sage or Palo Santo.

Crystal allies. Keep special crystals to bless the altar space and raise the vibration of your altar.

Photos of ancestors and loved ones. Keeping photos of loved ones who have passed honors their memory, keeps the energy of their love close, and, if they are ancestors, invokes their protection and wisdom.

Candles. Light candles when honoring an ancestor, invoking connection to the Divine/Source/Universe/God/dess, or to activate the altar's energy.

Statues of deities that have meaning for you. Some people place statues that hold religious meaning on their altar; others may have statues of deities they work closely with.

A bowl for offering. This can be a bowl or other container that holds a fruit offering, water offering, or flower offering.

To keep living quarters free and clear of negative or stale energies, it's also ideal to keep a clean home. Do regular physical cleanings and keep clutter to a minimum, because dirt and dust also hold stagnant energy.

At the office, placing a few crystals by the computer, laptop, or mobile devices can help create a more balanced workspace. Especially useful is black tourmaline, because it blocks and absorbs electromagnetic pollution that computers and other electronics may give off.

In addition, setting up a workplace crystal grid is a great way to establish a protective field between ourselves and those we work with, especially if the work environment is toxic. Taking four each of black tourmaline, clear quartz, or selenite and putting each piece into the four corners of a workplace (or home, or even your bedframe) creates this effect.

In the next section, we'll cover various physical, emotional, mental, and spiritual ailments, symptoms, and experiences that appear in our bodies when our chakras are unbalanced, and study each chakra's healing techniques in detail.

II

HEALING YOUR CHAKRAS

In Part 2, you will apply your new knowledge and use self-healing techniques to address common maladies. Chapter 3 offers an overview of over forty symptoms and ailments associated with imbalanced chakras. Chapter 4 provides a range of different healing techniques that you can use to balance and heal your chakra system.

3

COMMON SYMPTOMS
AND AILMENTS

• • • • • •

Often, when something is "off," we'll experience the
first signals through emotional, mental, and spiritual
symptoms because they show up in the energy body
first. If they are not addressed while in the energy
body, they become physical symptoms. In this chapter, we'll go through many common symptoms and
ailments in alphabetical order, as well as the affected
chakras. These can range from simple symptoms,
such as neck pain, to more complicated issues, like
addiction. Because a person may experience a particular symptom/ailment for different reasons, we'll
look at a number of possible explanations.

Addiction

CHAKRAS AFFECTED *mostly the throat chakra, but all other chakras are affected*

Addiction occurs when we become dependent on a legal or illegal drug, substance, food, or behavior. Long-standing addiction can cause serious problems for us in relationships, our physical, mental, and spiritual health, our work, and with the legal system. When we are suffering from addiction, we have lost communication with ourselves and others, feel silenced, and feel unable to express ourselves. These are all traits that involve an out-of-balance throat chakra.

Although addiction is mostly related to the throat chakra, other chakras may cause the addiction to occur or continue. When we feel ashamed about who we are, or self-medicate to avoid processing painful emotions, our sacral plexus chakra is involved. If feelings of low self-worth or powerlessness have played a big part in the addiction, our solar plexus chakra is involved. If we are in our addiction as a result of not feeling grounded, or feel like we must do it to survive, our root chakra may be crying out for help. If it is an attempt to quiet our broken heart, or we feel disconnected from ourselves, our heart chakra is at the root of our addiction. Our crown chakra is involved in addiction when we feel disconnected from the Divine and feel alone in the world.

Lastly, sometimes the third eye chakra's ability to perceive more than what is in our physical line of sight (such as having psychic abilities or trusting that which we do not yet know or understand) can be part of a person's addiction; the addictive behavior may be an effort to numb these psychic abilities, because an individual may find them scary or not understand them.

Adrenal Fatigue

CHAKRA AFFECTED *root chakra, sacral plexus chakra*

Adrenal fatigue happens when we are exposed to chronic stress. Our adrenal glands become taxed by the constant heightened stress response, rendering adrenal health insufficient. Under normal circumstances, the adrenal glands trigger the release of cortisol (otherwise known as the stress hormone), which steps in to help us handle stress. Adrenaline, our fight-or-flight hormone, is also put in motion by our adrenals. Both of these hormones are activated to help us get out of stressful situations. This is great when used on a short-term basis. However, those suffering from adrenal fatigue have been running on empty as a result of a chronic stress response.

Some signs of adrenal fatigue include general tiredness, body aches, unexplained weight loss, low blood pressure, lightheadedness, loss of body hair, and skin discoloration (hyperpigmentation). Because the adrenals are the glands of the root chakra and the sacral plexus chakra, any issues around adrenal fatigue, in addition to addressing the cause(s) of stress themselves, should be explored. Because the root chakra deals with issues around feeling secure, grounded, and stable, it is worth exploring areas of unbalance in our lives. It's also worth exploring issues around power and self-esteem, which are traits related to the sacral plexus chakra.

Anger

CHAKRAS AFFECTED *mostly root chakra, but other chakras are affected*

Anger, by itself, is a healthy emotion. It helps us stand up for ourselves, create healthy boundaries, initiate action and change, and escape harmful situations. However, when it is unexpressed, channeled in unhealthy ways, or harms ourselves or others, it can cause discord in our lives.

When we are angry over a situation or at someone, the root is often fear—fear that our safety, livelihood, or survival is being threatened. Because of this, anger often resonates with the root chakra, which is our survival chakra.

But fear turning into anger can affect the other chakras, too. For instance, our crown chakra may need balancing if we feel like we've been dealt a bad hand in life and are angry at the Divine/Source/Universe/God/dess for the perceived injustice. Our third eye chakra may be involved if we are not in touch with our emotional intelligence, we're unable to trust beyond what we can physically see (such as being frustrated with a current situation without seeing the bigger picture, nor trusting that we have options other than what's in front of us), and we rely only on our intellect. If we feel triggered into anger by being silenced or unable to express ourselves, our throat chakra is out of harmony. If our anger is due to feeling like our heart has been trampled on, we're focused on past hurts, we feel lonely, or we find it hard to forgive, our heart chakra needs healing. If we are angry because we have been placed in an unhealthy power dynamic (like dealing with toxic coworkers or an unhealthy relationship), or if we feel things are out of control in our lives, our solar plexus chakra is out of balance.

Lastly, our sacral plexus chakra might be out of balance if our creativity is being stifled or our emotions are repressed. Our anger can be simmering and may eventually blow up, unexpectedly. Our anger will also come from here when we have experienced sexual abuse, or feel our sexuality has been threatened.

Anorexia and Bulimia

CHAKRA AFFECTED *solar plexus chakra*

Anorexia is an eating disorder characterized by abnormally low body weight, a distorted perception of one's weight, and intense fear of gaining weight. Individuals suffering from anorexia severely restrict the amount of food they eat. Bulimia, on the other hand, is when a person binges (or eats large amounts of food), followed by an episode of purging—often through forced vomiting, taking laxatives, or doing unhealthy levels of exercise. Because both eating disorders are about harshly judging one's physical appearance, equating thinness with self-worth, and trying to control one's own self-image to correct perceived physical flaws, anorexia and bulimia both result in an out-of-balance solar plexus chakra, the power center for issues around control, self-esteem, and confidence.

Anxiety

CHAKRAS AFFECTED *all chakras, depending on what type of anxiety*

Occasional anxiety is often a part of regular day-to-day life. However, when a feeling of intense, excessive, and persistent worry permeates our everyday existence, it can be debilitating. For some who suffer from anxiety, it can peak into fear or terror within minutes, causing a panic attack (see Panic Attacks, page 74). Oftentimes, it can interfere with our quality of life.

Depending on what kind of anxiety you may have, any of the chakras may be involved. For instance, the crown chakra being out of balance may cause anxiety if we feel like the Divine/Source/Universe/God/dess does not have our back. If our anxiety is caused by an imbalance in the third eye chakra, it is usually because we do not trust our own intuition, and feel anxious about the unknown. If it is caused by a throat chakra that is out of harmony, we are anxious about expressing ourselves, communicating with others, and saying how we really feel. If we are holding onto past hurts, or, conversely, if we are anxious because we are disconnected from our feelings, our heart chakra may be out of balance. If we feel anxious because we are simply overwhelmed by everything, feel intimidated, feel caught in some kind of power dynamic in a relationship, or feel pressure to perform well in our lives, our out-of-balance solar plexus chakra is causing our anxiety. If our sacral plexus chakra is involved, guilt or shame is propelling our anxiety, usually over intense emotions that haven't been fully processed. This also happens when there's anxiety related to past trauma, especially sexual trauma. If we are feeling anxious about our material survival in this world (food, shelter, money, and so on), our root chakra is out of balance, making us feel like we are in constant survival mode.

Asthma and Allergies

CHAKRA AFFECTED *heart chakra*

When we experience narrowing airways, and they produce extra mucous, it can trigger coughing, wheezing, and shortness of breath. When we have allergies, our immune system makes antibodies that identify a specific allergen as harmful, even if it may not be. Both conditions can affect one's quality of life. Oftentimes, these conditions are due to a compromised immune system and may cause respiratory distress and inflammation in our skin, airway, sinuses, or digestive system. But, because they are in the realm of the heart chakra, sometimes these types of physical reactions can be linked to an imbalance in that chakra, particularly if we are having issues around grief, heartache, love, and compassion.

Back Pain

Pain in any area of the back—upper back, middle back, or lower back—that hasn't been caused by physical trauma or repetitive physical stress may be saying something about chakra health. Pain can range from a dull chronic ache that keeps the back tight to sharp acute pain that limits range of motion.

UPPER BACK

CHAKRAS AFFECTED *throat chakra, heart chakra*

Sometimes, when we are not speaking our truth or when we are experiencing heartbreak, a threat to self-love, or difficulty in love with others, the resulting tension can actually manifest physically as tension or pain in the upper back. We may also be feeling unsupported, unloved, or that we are holding back love.

MIDDLE BACK

CHAKRAS AFFECTED *heart chakra, solar plexus chakra*

When we have issues around love, feeling loved, holding onto past hurts, or feeling challenged in our power, we may experience tension or pain in the middle back. Sometimes this happens because we are stuck in those past feelings, and may feel racked with a sense of guilt over what we have done or said to create a situation.

LOWER BACK

CHAKRAS AFFECTED *sacral plexus chakra, root chakra*

When we are feeling challenged in our abundance, relationships, creative expression; holding back emotions or simply not processing them; having issues around survival and obtaining the basic necessities, we may suffer tension and pain in the lower back. We may especially have back pain (not due to physical trauma) when we feel financially unsupported.

Cancer

CHAKRAS AFFECTED *all*

Cancer occurs when abnormal cells develop and divide uncontrollably, infiltrating and destroying normal body tissue. It can happen on many different levels, and the symptoms vary depending on which parts of the body are affected. Some symptoms include fatigue, weight changes, skin changes, palpable lumps or areas of thickening under the skin, unexplained and persistent muscle or joint pain, and unexplained and persistent fevers or night sweats, among others. Factors known to increase risk of cancer include age, habits, family history, health conditions, and environment. However, the Mayo Clinic states that the majority of cancers occur in people who don't have any known risk factors at all. In terms of energy, cancer can be the result of long-standing resentment and deep hurt that has been left unprocessed, ignored, or denied, manifesting in carrying hatred, grief, or other toxic emotion that eats away the self.

These can manifest on many levels, and as a result of imbalance in various chakras:

- Brain tumors: Crown chakra
- Lung cancer: Throat and heart chakras
- Cancers of thyroid, larynx, and esophagus: Throat chakra
- Breast cancer: Heart chakra
- Cancers of stomach, liver, intestines, and pancreas: Solar plexus chakra
- Cancers of cervix, ovaries, uterus, colon, and rectum: chakra
- Prostate and rectal cancer: Sacral plexus and root chakras

Codependency

CHAKRAS AFFECTED *root chakra, heart chakra, solar plexus chakra, sacral plexus chakra*

When we are in a dysfunctional, one-sided relationship—where we rely on our partner excessively for most of our emotional and psychological needs—we are said to be codependent. Codependency also describes a relationship that enables another person's irresponsible behavior or addiction, where one partner regularly sacrifices their needs and wants to help the other, to the point of giving up parts of themselves, having poor boundaries and low self-esteem, feeling insecure, and poorly communicating painful emotions. Because codependent relationships are often based on the fear of abandonment and rejection, there is a direct link to the root chakra, where fear-based actions and feelings stem from.

Codependency often arises from childhood, when a dysfunctional family ignores or denies pain, fear, anger, or shame. This can include when a family member is dealing with addiction; when there is physical, emotional, or sexual abuse; or if a family member is suffering from a chronic mental or physical illness. Issues stemming from unresolved family pain are also related to the root chakra.

With codependency, there is also an imbalance in the heart chakra, mainly because we are focused on our love toward others rather than our love for ourselves, which is often set aside. It's a type of disconnect from our heart center. When this chakra is out of balance, it can also lead to a lack of discernment in relationships.

Because our self-esteem is challenged as a result of, and upon entering, a codependent relationship, our solar plexus chakra is also affected. If our sacral plexus chakra is unbalanced, then any feelings regarding shame, guilt, anger, and resentment will surface in a codependent relationship, as well as a lack of healthy boundaries.

Conflict

CHAKRA AFFECTED *throat chakra, sometimes solar plexus chakra and sacral plexus chakra*

When we are in conflict with someone or something, and we disagree with what is happening or what someone is telling us, there is a disagreement on what is being expressed. Whenever we have an issue around expression and communication, the throat chakra is involved. Sometimes we may avoid conflict altogether, which is a version of silencing ourselves. When we silence ourselves, we become resentful, and the uncommunicated feelings remain pent up within, until we finally explode (see Anger, page 56). Whether we seek conflict, avoid it, or simply find ourselves within it, our throat chakra is trying to be heard. We are trying to be heard, express ourselves, and communicate what we really feel.

Conflict may also be a sign that our our solar plexus chakra needs attention, since conflict can indicate that our personal power is being challenged, or that our sacral plexus chakra is involved since the sacral plexus chakra is the seat of our emotions.

Constipation

CHAKRAS AFFECTED *root chakra, possibly solar plexus chakra*

Difficult or infrequent bowel movements may indicate constipation. Because the rectum and anus are at the level of the root chakra, any dysfunctions involving these parts of our bodies can indicate that our root chakra is out of balance. It may be helpful to consider whether you are feeling triggered with survival issues that are causing stress—primal needs like having food to eat, water to drink, clothes to wear, a home to sleep in, and feeling safe and secure. Because constipation is physically a result of an imbalanced digestive system, it would also be helpful to make sure the solar plexus chakra is balanced. Experiences of fear, lack of confidence, lack of self-respect, and difficulty feeling in touch with our power may also affect the digestive process, creating colon or intestinal problems and other disorders. As a result, an imbalance in the solar plexus chakra may contribute to a root chakra's constipation issue.

Depression

CHAKRAS AFFECTED *crown chakra, heart chakra*

Depression can happen for a number of reasons. Sometimes it passes through temporarily. Other times, it can be a constant presence in our lives. Oftentimes, for those who suffer from chronic depression, it can be debilitating. Depression can feel like persistent sadness, emptiness, or hopelessness, the absence of pleasure in day-to-day activities, and as though life at times is not worth living. It can also affect our appetite and our sleep—either keeping us up, or making us need too much sleep. Sometimes there will even be recurrent thoughts about death or suicide.

When we are depressed, one of the main root causes is a deep feeling of loneliness. This is why depression is mainly linked to the crown chakra. When we feel connected to the rest of the world, and the Divine, our crown chakra is open and balanced. When we feel disconnected from the world, and even have anger toward the Divine at how our life has unfolded, it is usually an indication that our energy in this chakra is out of harmony. In addition, an unbalanced heart chakra may cause depression, due to lack of connection with ourselves.

Digestive Issues

CHAKRA AFFECTED *solar plexus chakra*

When we have difficulty digesting problems that arise in our physical lives, we feel it energetically, too. If you've ever lost your appetite, or conversely, had a ravenous one as a response to stress or overwhelming news, you already understand the effects of the solar plexus chakra. Because this chakra is our power center, when we feel challenged in our power—such as feeling low self-esteem, intimidation, or powerlessness—this chakra becomes imbalanced. And, because of this, digestive issues can result.

Disconnection from Self and Others

CHAKRA AFFECTED *heart chakra*

When we are disconnected from who we are, from how we feel, and from our dreams, passions, and what lights us up, our heart chakra is out of balance. Oftentimes, this first displays as frustration with not feeling connected with others. We may find ourselves spending long periods of time by ourselves, but not in a way that rejuvenates our spirit or helps us feel connected with ourselves. It's usually accompanied with a general feeling of malaise or discontent about life. We want to feel joyful, but don't, or are not in touch with what makes us happy. Sometimes, we may be depressed, which often happens when we are disconnected from ourselves. We all want to connect—with ourselves and with others. It is hardwired into our human existence. People who are fully disconnected from themselves may not even be aware that they are. They may be fully entrenched in their daily schedule, living on autopilot or in survival mode, not from a place of gratefulness, engagement with who they are, or connection and awareness of how their daily activities make them feel. Those who are able to create awareness around their daily activities, and even do quick check-ins with themselves during the day, are more able to create a connection with themselves, and can begin a more healthy connection with the heart chakra.

Fatigue

CHAKRAS AFFECTED *solar plexus chakra, crown chakra*

When exhaustion is ongoing, increases, or isn't relieved by rest, there is a constant state of weariness, and our energy reserves feel depleted. This affects concentration, focus, energy, and motivation, which eventually impacts us energetically. If we are the type who's prone to adrenal fatigue, addicted to being busy, or habitually overwork ourselves, we are driving ourselves into fatigue due to solar plexus chakra imbalance.

Fatigue is related to the solar plexus chakra, our power center. When we link our self-esteem and self-confidence to our performance in the workplace or in life, we take it very personally if a project fails or appears to be subpar. We then work ourselves into a frenzy to meet a perception of perfection, which results in fatigue. On the other hand, if our fatigue is due to depression or feeling disconnected from the Divine, the crown chakra is in need of balancing.

Fear

CHAKRAS AFFECTED *root chakra, solar plexus chakra*

When we feel fear, we perceive someone or something as dangerous— we feel it is going to cause us harm or is threatening our existence. Fear causes a change in brain and organ function, activating a cascade within our sympathetic nervous system that brings us into fight-or-flight mode. It is an adaptive behavior that helps us identify threats, and survive predators and natural disasters. Fear is helpful for survival. However, being in this state for too long can negatively impact our lives. Some issues that can trigger this primal reaction are around basic survival needs and feeling secure in our lives, neighborhoods, and families.

Anytime our basic needs are threatened, it creates an imbalance in the root chakra. And, if we've been taught at an early age to stay in this fear, it can create long-standing root chakra disharmonies that affect us as adults. Staying in fear for long periods of time can also affect our hormonal system and cause adrenal fatigue (see Adrenal Fatigue).

Another chakra that can be affected when we feel fear is our solar plexus chakra. This is often a result of the initial root chakra imbalance. Not feeling supported in our basic needs can create a sense of powerlessness and challenge our self-esteem, both of which are related to the solar plexus chakra.

Grief

CHAKRA AFFECTED *heart chakra*

It is healthy to grieve when we lose someone or something precious. However, if the grief is left unprocessed, if we deny that it exists, or if we hold onto it past its usefulness in an unhealthy way, it can cause a block in the heart chakra. If left unchecked, the imbalance caused by holding onto grief for too long will cause us to feel lonely, lose hope, or cultivate bitterness. While grieving, there may be a tendency to isolate ourselves. This, too, can serve a purpose, because some of us need the downtime to decompress and process how we're feeling. However, because our heart chakra connects us to our self-love and love for others, if we isolate ourselves for too long, our heart chakra suffers from lack of connection. We need to remember to reconnect, not only with ourselves, but with other people. Although it may feel permanent, everything transforms and changes, including our perception that we are forever torn apart from those we love.

Guilt

CHAKRAS AFFECTED *sacral plexus chakra, solar plexus chakra*

Guilt is the feeling of having done something wrong, whether the perception is true or not. This emotion is often related to the sacral plexus chakra, which is the seat of our emotions. This energy center is also associated with pleasure and the emotions of our sexuality. If we were taught to repress our sexuality and/or emotions growing up, we often feel guilt and shame in our adult life (see Shame, page 77). Guilt is meant to help us keep things in check. But, usually, this is an unproductive emotion that blocks us from receiving pleasure, and healthy pleasure is what we experience when our sacral plexus chakra is balanced. Because guilt can impact our self-esteem and our sense of power, our solar plexus chakra can also be affected. A big part of healing this, other than the sacral plexus and solar plexus chakra remedies listed in this book, is to allow ourselves to feel our feelings, rather than deny them or push them down.

Headache

CHAKRAS AFFECTED *third eye chakra, crown chakra*

When we get headaches that aren't directly caused by physical imbalances, it can be an indication that there is disharmony in one of our chakras. When you have frontal headaches, with symptoms such as sinus pressure and pressure behind your eyes that can spread to your forehead, it is often a third eye chakra disharmony. This kind of headache may indicate that we are focusing only on our intellect, fearing the spiritual aspects of ourselves, only able to see the physical reality in life and not trusting our intuition. Sometimes, when these headaches occur, it is because we are ignoring the inner wisdom we possess. When we receive intuitive "hints" but don't act on them, we are not honoring our third eye wisdom. For example, perhaps you feel you should pursue a new opportunity, but don't. Or you experience an intuitive knowing that a certain person may not be healthy to interact with, but you enter into a relationship with them anyway. Acting in opposition to intuitive hints can cause discord and an imbalance with your third eye chakra.

If, on the other hand, you have a vertex headache (one that is at the top center of the head), it may be caused by an imbalanced crown chakra. This may indicate difficulty trusting life or our path, seeing the larger pattern or picture, or cultivating faith in ourselves and our connection to the Divine. We may also feel alone or unsatisfied with life.

Hemorrhoids

CHAKRA AFFECTED *root chakra*

Hemorrhoids, otherwise known as piles, are swollen veins in the anus and lower rectum. They may be found under the skin around the anus (external hemorrhoids), or inside the rectum (internal hemorrhoids), and are similar to varicose veins. If they're not caused by straining during bowel movements, increased pressure on the veins during pregnancy, or one of many other physical causes, they may be caused by a chakra imbalance.

Because the lower rectum and anus are at the level of the root chakra, any dysfunction that involves these parts of our bodies can indicate that our root chakra is out of balance. This chakra is all about survival, so primal needs like having food to eat, water to drink, clothes to wear, a roof over our heads, and feeling safe and secure in our lives may arise. Hemorrhoids may also be energetically linked to a fear of letting go, anger of the past, or feeling burdened.

Hip Pain

CHAKRA AFFECTED *sacral plexus chakra*

When we experience issues in the hips (such as tightness, tension, muscle spasms, or pain), that aren't the result of physical trauma to the area or overexercising, there is often a relationship to sacral plexus chakra issues. Often, the hips can hold a lot of unexpressed emotions, usually emotions that haven't been dealt with, or that we've been avoiding.

Because the sacral plexus chakra is the seat of our emotions, we cause an imbalance in this area when we do not honor our feelings around a situation. In addition, if we are feeling issues around expressing healthy sexuality, particularly around shame related to our sexuality (another marker for a sacral plexus chakra imbalance), this can also cause tightness or pain in the hips.

Infertility

CHAKRAS AFFECTED *sacral plexus chakra, root chakra, solar plexus chakra*

When a woman is unable to conceive despite frequent attempts for at least a year, this is considered infertility. Although many experience infertility, the frustration and fear that women trying to conceive experience creates much stress, sometimes even shame. The sacral plexus chakra is involved here, not only because it is associated with the womb and genitals, but also because it is the seat of our emotions.

Many people who are dealing with infertility battle through severe emotions, making them wonder: "Is this the right decision?" "Do I even want to be a parent?" "Am I with the right partner?" "What if I'm not a good parent?" and "How will this change my life?"

Sometimes, a physical cause or causes—such as poor egg quality, low sperm count, lack of menstruation, high follicle-stimulating hormone (FSH), or other issues—are to blame. But many other times, there is the component of high stress on the part of the people trying to conceive. Because infertility can trigger issues around family, the root chakra is also involved. Other root chakra considerations for people trying to conceive arise if they are trying to build a family when they're not receiving support from significant family members, or if they're concerned about passing on undesirable family traits to their offspring. And, because creating a new life can challenge one's self-esteem, often making them feel powerless over their bodies, solar plexus chakra issues can result as well, because this energy center is our power center.

Jaw Pain/Temporomandibular Joint (TMJ) Pain

CHAKRA AFFECTED *throat chakra*

The temporomandibular joint (TMJ) connects your jawbone to your skull, and acts like a sliding hinge to open and close the mouth. We have one joint on each side of our jaw. Sometimes pain in the area can result from a jaw injury, arthritis, genetics, or teeth clenching and grinding. Teeth grinding, or bruxism, can often be due to stress that is held in the jaw. It can also occur when we're trying to hold back what we really want to say or feel silenced, which is related to our throat chakra. Acupuncture, massaging the masseter muscle (the muscle in your jaw that controls chewing), and wearing a mouthguard at night can be helpful for the physical aspects of TMJ pain.

TMJ pain may also be rooted in an energetic component—feeling like we're not able to speak up for ourselves, say what we mean, or communicate effectively. TMJ pain can also result when we're feeling resentful. To address the full picture of jaw pain relief, we not only need to examine sources for physical relief, but understand the possible energetic causes as well. If you find yourself biting your tongue when you really want to say something, or you're clenching your jaw tightly to hold yourself back, it may be worthwhile to examine what you are holding in your throat chakra, and why you are finding it difficult to say what's on your mind.

Leg Pain

CHAKRAS AFFECTED *root chakra, solar plexus chakra*

Leg pain, when not directly related to physical trauma, is often linked to a root chakra imbalance. Sometimes, leg pain can symbolize our resistance toward moving forward in life, which can manifest as self-sabotaging behaviors based on fear—fear that we'll fail, or fear that we'll actually get what we want and step into our power. If this is the case, the root chakra imbalance can also be linked to the solar plexus chakra. But, it's mostly a root chakra issue if the resistance to moving forward is due to fear around bills, or gaining or losing housing, food, water, or clothing.

Loneliness

CHAKRA AFFECTED *heart chakra*

When we feel lonely, we are under the impression that we are not connected to anyone. This is a powerful feeling, and a powerful illusion. Our heart chakra teaches us that we are all geared to love and to connect with each other (yes, even those of us who attest to being loners!). Love is the real deal, and anything resembling fear (such as loneliness, which is feeling disconnected or the fear of being disconnected) is not. We all need to connect. Our heart chakra wants us to connect, not only with ourselves—the most important connection of all—but with other people. When we are truly, deeply lonely, it is often because the connection with ourselves has been lost. This is the realm of the heart chakra.

If you are feeling lonely, it may be because the heart chakra is out of balance, and you may have closed yourself off from love, whether as a reaction to being hurt after opening your heart or because you feel you don't deserve love. When we find it difficult to show ourselves loving kindness, such as taking the time to do daily tasks, performing self-care rituals like resting when needed, eating foods that fuel our system in healthy ways, and surrounding ourselves with uplifting people, it is difficult for our heart to radiate with joy. When we fully and completely love ourselves, and are connected with our heart chakra, we are never truly lonely, no matter what our circumstances.

Neck Pain

CHAKRA AFFECTED *throat chakra*

Neck pain that is not caused by physical trauma or bodily harm (like an accident) can be the result of imbalanced throat chakra energy related to the way we interact with the world. When we fail to express ourselves in a very honest or open way, or when we try to hide certain parts of ourselves, such as fear or insecurity, from other people, it creates imbalances in the throat chakra. Examples of this behavior might be pretending to be happy in a relationship when deep down you're dissatisfied, or holding yourself back from speaking openly at work. There may be a range of reasons why we hold ourselves back, but the result is usually the same—neck pain caused by an inability to express ourselves freely and openly.

Neuropathy

CHAKRA AFFECTED *third eye chakra*

Neuropathy, or feeling pain throughout the body or in a specific area of the body, is usually caused by damage to the nerves. This is often the result of a traumatic injury, infection, diabetes, side effects of chemotherapy, inherited causes, or exposure to toxins. However, if the cause is not due to neurological injury, it may be the result of an imbalanced third eye chakra, because this chakra can be involved with neurological disturbances. An example of this is experiencing pain in the body after feeling disconnected from our intuition, or fearing the spiritual aspects of ourselves. Oftentimes, fear of our spiritual self can indicate that we are either on the verge of becoming more connected with our inner wisdom, or that we actually have a very strong intuition and are afraid of our power. So, if neuropathy is caused by energetic blockage, this may be exhibited by being able to only focus on the intellect and logical mind, rejecting any spiritual perspectives we may have, and focusing only on what is physically in front of us—all of which are aspects of an unbalanced third eye chakra.

Panic Attacks

CHAKRAS AFFECTED *heart chakra, solar plexus chakra, root chakra*

Panic attacks occur when we are gripped by sudden, acute, and disabling anxiety. They are often accompanied by palpitations, a pounding heart, increased heart rate, sweating, trembling, shaking, shortness of breath, and a feeling of impending doom. These debilitating attacks can occur when we are disconnected from our heart chakra, and are not listening to what it's trying to tell us. In addition, our root chakra is involved when panic and fear set in, because our primal fear for our own survival can be triggered. With our heart chakra feeling disconnected and our fear mechanisms in play, our power center at the solar plexus chakra can feel like we've been punched in the gut, because our self-esteem and sense of confidence resides there.

Sciatica

CHAKRAS AFFECTED *root chakra, sacral plexus chakra*

Sciatica is a pain condition that radiates from the lower back, through the hips and buttocks, and down each leg. When it's not caused by trauma to the spine, or some other injury, sciatic pain can reflect an imbalanced root chakra. The root chakra deals with issues around survival and being. When primal issues arise, like where you're getting your next meal, if you're going to be able to make your rent, if your children will be provided for, or if you generally live in fear that all the basic things in life may be easily snatched away, then your root chakra is not in harmony.

In addition, sciatica can energetically symbolize fear of money and the future. Anytime we have issues with pain that limits how we walk in this world, literally and figuratively, we need to ask ourselves if we are purposely limiting our progress to move forward in life, or if we are living in fear of the next steps that we may need to take to accomplish our goals.

Sometimes when we experience sciatic pain, it may be because we feel unsafe in this world. The sacral plexus chakra is related to the lower vertebrae, pelvis, and hip area, so it may be worth examining whether or not we are connecting with and honoring our emotions, if we are freely expressing ourselves creatively, and if we are able to allow ourselves to enjoy pleasure in life.

Self-Hate

CHAKRAS AFFECTED *heart chakra, root chakra, solar plexus chakra*

Self-hate is based on the perception that we are unlovable—that we do not deserve love due to doing something we perceive as terrible, or because when we were younger we were taught we were unlovable. Believing we are unlovable is a direct result of disconnection from our heart chakra. The heart chakra is all about love—love and compassion for ourselves and for others—and love always begins within.

If we hate ourselves, which is a learned behavior based on outdated perceptions, we need to see how we came to believe that. In addition, hate is an angry energy and emotion. And anger always stems from fear. Fear of our existence and the inability to stand up for ourselves are based in the root chakra. Fear related to self-hate can also reside in the solar plexus chakra, if it is fear due to lack of self-esteem. If this chakra is unbalanced, our power center is challenged, and we may feel a lack of confidence. In feeling powerless, fearful of existing, and disconnected from our heart chakra, we can easily believe outdated perceptions that we are unloveable. The good news is outdated perceptions are updateable, and energy can shift very quickly to recalibrate.

Sexual Abuse

CHAKRAS AFFECTED *sacral plexus chakra, root chakra, solar plexus chakra, throat chakra*

When we are sexually violated, the abuse can be very damaging, not only to our physical body, but to our soul as well. Because of the trauma, survivors of sexual abuse may shut down their feelings or disassociate from themselves to avoid feeling deep pain. They may feel ashamed, and possibly blame themselves for what happened (even though the trauma was in no way their fault). Their sexuality and feelings around pleasure may shift. And because, in that moment, a power dynamic was exploited, control issues may result. Rage around the incident, toward themselves, and/or their abuser, is often bottled up. These reactions are all understandable, given the depth of the trauma, and are all related to the sacral plexus chakra.

If the sexual abuse was perpetrated by a family member, and if important family members were unsupportive after learning of the trauma, feelings of betrayal may arise, which are connected to the root chakra. In addition, if the pain remains unprocessed, it may affect overall self-confidence and self-esteem, which are related to the solar plexus chakra. The throat chakra can also be directly affected as a result of the violation, and survivors may feel silenced and unable to speak up (or at least feel uncomfortable doing so). The irony is that exercising the throat chakra, such as speaking up and sharing our stories, can be therapeutic—not only for the survivor, but also for others who need to hear their story. Sharing the emotion with those you feel safe with can feel very scary, but can ultimately open the door toward healing.

Shame

CHAKRAS AFFECTED *sacral plexus chakra, solar plexus chakra*

We experience shame when we feel humiliated—about something we perceive that we've done wrong, or something that somehow reflects the idea that we are inadequate, not good enough, or not strong enough. Sometimes we can feel shame about who we are, how we perform in front of others, when we feel defeated, and when it comes to how we feel about ourselves sexually. All of these strong feelings destabilize the sacral plexus chakra, which is the seat of our emotions. In fact, because this energy center is also where we house feelings about sex and sexuality, patients commonly experience shame around their bodies. Because shame can affect our personal power and how we see ourselves (often diminishing our own self-worth as a form of self-punishment for any perceived wrongs), the solar plexus chakra also takes a hit, and self-esteem is taxed.

Sinus Pain

CHAKRA AFFECTED *third eye chakra*

If you're experiencing pain in your sinuses unrelated to allergies, environmental irritants, or direct trauma, you may have an imbalance in your third eye chakra. Our sixth chakra is related to our inner sight—our intuition beyond physical evidence. It helps us trust beyond that which we can physically see, and allows us to follow our precious insight.

Oftentimes, sinus pain can be an energetic indication that we are irritated with someone who is close to us, and we may view the situation as full of discord. If this is the case, consider examining whether the relationship is still a healthy one. On the other hand, the problem could be the way the relationship is viewed, or because you might be operating from outdated perceptions of what is happening in the relationship.

Sexually Transmitted Infections (STIs)

CHAKRA AFFECTED *sacral plexus chakra*

If there are recurring sexually transmitted infections and diseases, there may be an imbalance in the sacral plexus chakra. This chakra deals with our perceptions of our sexuality, particularly how we express it, and the emotional aspects (versus the physical aspects). Oftentimes, shame plays a major part in recurring STIs, and it is no coincidence that when we perceive ourselves as promiscuous and feel great shame around it, STIs reoccur. This may be an indication that we need to unpack or question our perceptions about what we feel are healthy forms of sexual expression; we might want to look at whether or not our sexual perceptions of ourselves are accurate or outdated. Oftentimes, they are outdated, and we are still operating from old shame we are harboring from the past. Sometimes, there is also physical, emotional, or sexual abuse that colors the perception of ourselves as sexual beings. When we are able to heal our views about our sexual selves in healthy ways, we also heal our sacral plexus chakra.

Skin Issues

CHAKRA AFFECTED *crown chakra*

Our skin is our largest organ, and can manifest many disorders, including acne, eczema, psoriasis, rosacea, rashes, and dermatitis, among others. Although skin issues can surface as a result of poor diet, stress, hormonal issues, and skincare regimens, they can also surface as a result of an imbalanced crown chakra. If this is the case, it is worth examining any areas in your life where you feel disconnected from your spirituality and the Divine, and if you feel challenged by a lack of trust in the Divine or life.

Stomach Pain and Disorders

CHAKRA AFFECTED *solar plexus chakra*

Stomach pain and disorders can come in many forms: ulcers, constipation, diarrhea, inflammatory bowel syndrome (IBS), colon/intestinal problems, indigestion, acid reflux, and gastritis, among others. Aside from eating something that directly inflames our digestive tract, stomach pain can also result from feeling overwhelmed, out of control, powerless, intimidated, or lacking in self-respect. What we take in through our power center (our solar plexus chakra) is a way for us to digest our surroundings and take in our environment.

For example, I once knew a patient who experienced episodes of acid reflux after her divorce. In this case, her body was expressing the "acidic" emotion of resentment that the experience gave her. It was difficult for her to digest her divorce, which had made her feel powerless and out of control.

Our bodies are always telling us exactly where our imbalances lie, and digestive disorders are no exception.

Stress

CHAKRAS AFFECTED *root chakra, the other chakras can also be affected*

Stress, when referring to chakra health, is a state of mental tension and emotional strain resulting from very demanding circumstances and problems that occur in our lives, work situations, and relationships. When we experience stress, cortisol (otherwise known as our stress hormone) steps in to help us handle our stress. Adrenaline is our fight-or-flight hormone. Both of these hormones are activated by our adrenals to help us get out of stressful situations. This is great when used on a short-term basis. But, oftentimes, people can stay in stress response mode on a much longer-term basis. Whether short term or long term, stress can indicate an imbalanced root chakra, because this energy center is related to our personal security, feeling safe, and feeling like all aspects of our survival are met (such as having food to eat, a roof over our head, and clothes to wear). When the root chakra is out of balance, we are operating from a place of fear; we feel unsafe, like our needs are not met. Our survival instincts are activated. Because the primal feeling of instability and fear can affect other chakras, stress can affect our chakras in the following ways:

- Crown chakra: Stress from feeling alone and disconnected from the Divine
- Third eye chakra: Stress from not being able to trust what's coming next in our lives, or from being unable to see the bigger picture in front of us
- Throat chakra: Stress from feeling like we're not expressing ourselves the way we'd like, or that we're not being heard in the way we want to be heard; stress around speaking our truth
- Heart chakra: Stress stemming from disconnection with self and, as a result, with others
- Solar plexus chakra: Stress coming from lack of self-worth and a sense of powerlessness
- Sacral plexus chakra: Stress from pent-up emotions, not expressing ourselves creatively or in healthy sexual ways
- Root chakra: Stress from feeling like our basic needs are not being met

Thyroid Disorders

CHAKRA AFFECTED *throat chakra*

The throat chakra is all about speaking our truth. When we say what we mean, mean what we say, express how we really feel, and communicate in ways that are aligned with who we are, we honor our throat chakra. If we have disorders that involve the neck, such as imbalances in the thyroid, that lack direct medical explanation, it is likely the throat chakra is imbalanced. It is possible that we have silenced ourselves, usually in regards to something traumatic (such as abuse), or something we feel unable to express. Even if not due to experiencing trauma, thyroid disorders can simply be a symptom of habitually staying silent when there is much we want to say. Those who've had these kinds of thyroid disorders due to abuse, then heal and release the pain they've been holding onto, tend to be very effective at communicating who they are with others, often beginning with sharing their own story in healing ways.

Uterine Fibroids and Cysts

CHAKRA AFFECTED *sacral plexus chakra*

According to the Mayo Clinic, uterine fibroids are noncancerous growths of the uterus that often appear during childbearing years. Many women have uterine fibroids sometime during their lives. Sometimes they don't cause any symptoms. However, at other times, they can grow to a significant size and cause pain during menstruation, when you're having a bowel movement, or when your body is trying to digest food—they can even affect your breathing. Cysts are fluid-filled sacs inside, or within, the ovaries.

When there is abnormal growth within the uterus, it is often a signal that the sacral plexus chakra is out of balance. Because there are actual blockages in the reproductive area, the energy body is telling you that there is blocked creative flow and energy within. You may be holding onto old, negative, and toxic thoughts, emotions, or feelings that are flowing life energy into dead ends. These might be jobs or relationships that you've outgrown, or conflicts about creativity, abundance, reproduction, and/or relationships in your life.

Weight Issues

CHAKRAS AFFECTED *root chakra, solar plexus chakra, sacral plexus chakra*

Although weight issues are often addressed with behavioral, lifestyle, exercise, and dietary changes, another possible cause is a lack of feeling grounded. When we do not feel grounded, this is a root chakra problem. A balanced root chakra helps us feel connected to nature. It also makes us feel secure—that no matter what we may be experiencing in life, all of our basic needs are met. What we often do to feel more grounded is gain weight.

Another possibility is that we sometimes put a buffer of weight between us and the world when we feel attacked, intimidated, or our self-esteem feels off. In this case, the cause may be more of an imbalanced solar plexus chakra, which is our power center.

Sometimes, feeling our emotions and being in touch with pleasure can be difficult for us. When we bottle up our feelings about what's going on around us and within us, do not process our emotions that may have shaped our feelings around worth and survival, and do not experience the pleasure of eating, then our sacral plexus chakra may be unbalanced.

This chapter looked at a long list of common symptoms and ailments, as well as their associated chakras. Next, we'll discuss a variety of ways to heal each of the different chakras.

4

HEALING REMEDIES AND TREATMENTS

· · · · · · ·

This chapter is divided into eight sections—one for each of the seven chakras, and a final section on healing multiple chakras. In each section, we'll cover some tried-and-true techniques that have helped me and my patients get in touch with each chakra. These practical techniques are tools to help you get started on your healing journey.

THE ROOT CHAKRA

The root chakra is all about being grounded, feeling secure that your basic needs are being met, and feeling connected to your family and tribal consciousness in healthy ways. The following meditations, crystal techniques, essential oil applications, and yoga postures will help you connect with what you may be holding in that chakra. Most importantly, they'll help you initiate connection with the energy vortex within you, so you may open into the wisdom it holds.

Meditations

Here's an easy, tried-and-true meditation and visualization to connect with the root chakra:

1. While sitting or lying comfortably, take three slow, deep breaths. Each time you inhale, imagine the breath energizing your perineum—the area between the genitals and the anus. Each time you exhale, release anything you may be holding in that area. This might be fears, pain, or even expectations of how you're supposed to feel while doing this meditation. Personally, I find that holding my hands over my heart as I meditate on each chakra helps me connect to the chakra I'm concentrating on more quickly. You may want to put one hand over the heart chakra, and the other hand over the pubic bone—the bony area where your pubic hair begins. Another hand position is placing both hands at the lower aspect of your hips.

2. "Wake up" the connection with the root chakra by gently tapping at the top of the pubic bone or both sides of your lower hips, or by gently massaging the area in a small, circular motion with your first two fingers.

3. With each following breath, inhaling and exhaling through the nose, continue directing your breath to your root chakra. Imagine a red sphere of light in that area, pulsing and growing larger. Those who identify most with male energy should whirl the sphere clockwise, and those who identify most with female energy should whirl the sphere counterclockwise.

4. As you drop deeper and deeper into a calmer state, ask your root chakra what it needs right now. Allow yourself a few more breaths to see if you receive any feedback. It could be in the form of a word, sound, song, image, color, feeling, or intuition. Then act on the feedback you get. If you don't have any yet, not to worry! It will come as you continue practicing.

5. If you don't receive any of the intuitive hints listed previously, but instead feel an awareness in that area, similar to a pulsing anywhere at your lower hips and even traveling down to your feet, you are connecting with your root chakra!

6. At the end of your meditation, take three slow, deep breaths, directing the energy of your inhale into the soles of your feet, to ground yourself. Gently open your eyes.

7. *Caution when doing this meditation/visualization:* Because this practice takes some time to cultivate, be patient with yourself. If you find yourself starting to feel pain in the lower back or legs, you are pushing yourself too hard. It's time to take a break and revisit when you're more rejuvenated. Also, as you perform your meditation, understand that even seasoned meditation practitioners get what's aptly termed monkey mind, where other thoughts begin to enter your mind and may momentarily distract you. Just take this as a chance to observe the thought without judgment, let it pass through, and gently bring yourself back to center.

Crystals

Ruby, garnet, black tourmaline, bloodstone, hematite, obsidian, onyx, red jasper, lodestone, smoky quartz, and fire agate are the crystals that resonate with the root chakra. (For images of these crystals, see the Appendix on page 158.)

To use crystals to connect with your root chakra, make sure that they are first cleansed from the energies of others who may have handled them before you, and that your intention for how they will be used is set. You can clean your crystals by:

- Smudging with white sage. Simply light the tip of a white sage bundle until it begins to smoke, blow out the flame, and hold your crystal in the rising smoke for a few seconds, setting the intention that you'll be using the crystal to help you connect with your root chakra. This is my favorite method, because after your cleanse your crystal, you can also cleanse your body by directing the smoke toward your chakras (and the rest of your body) with your free hand.

- Laying them out overnight under the moonlight to soak up the moonbeams.

- Running water over them or soaking them in salt water. When cleaning with water, use caution. Any stones that rate low on the Mohs hardness scale (a scale that helps identify mineral specimens and compares the resistance to being scratched) may get damaged or dissolve as a result.

Now that you've cleansed and charged your crystals, you can work with them in a few ways:

- Get into a comfortable seated or lying down position. Hold the crystal in your left hand—the receiving hand—so you can receive the crystal's healing energy. Notice what you pick up from the crystal. Does it feel like a throbbing in your hand? Like static prickles? Or do you just have a simple awareness of its energy? If you don't feel any of these things, that's okay. Sometimes it takes a while to create an awareness with a stone's energy. You may ask the crystal to help you connect with the wisdom of your root chakra. Allow your mind and heart to open to feedback in the way of images, colors, sounds, words, memories, emotions, or other impressions that may flow through. Keep in mind that working with crystals can take some getting used to. If your root chakra doesn't open into an epiphany right on the spot (which is unlikely on a first try, but anything is possible!), understand that you are still one step closer to being more connected with it. Be compassionate with yourself and know that it is on its way.

- Alternately, while lying down, place your selected root chakra crystal on top of your pubic bone. Take three slow and deep breaths. Allow yourself to drink in the energy of the crystal. As with the preceding holding technique, you may feel the energy in the area pulse, like a gentle heartbeat. You may feel a slight static energy traveling anywhere from your lower hips to your feet. Or you may have an awareness that the crystal's energy is interacting with your energy. If you don't feel any of these things, that's okay. Consider saying the affirmation listed in the last paragraph of the Essential Oils section to more intentionally connect with your root chakra.

Essential Oils

Myrrh, vetiver, sandalwood, patchouli, and spikenard are the essential oils that correspond with the root chakra.

To use a single oil (or a blend of oils) to help you connect with the root chakra, add 5 or 6 drops maximum per oil to a dime-size portion of carrier oil (such as jojoba oil). Usually, I recommend applying essential oils to the chakras themselves. However, because of the location and sensitivity of the skin in the root chakra area, it is better to activate the oils another way.

First, put the oil mixture in your hands and rub your hands together. Through the friction, you will release the scent and energy of the oils. Open your palms to release the fragrance. Deeply inhale the scent. Place your open palm over your pubic bone, allowing the energy of the oils to sink into the area. You might also try placing both hands at the lower aspect of your hips.

Whether you choose to anoint your root chakra directly, or activate the properties of the oils by rubbing them between your palms, take the time to intentionally create a connection with your root chakra. Say something like, "I now intend to create a connection with my root chakra. May I feel grounded and secure in my being and existence. I release all fear that keeps me from feeling safe in my life. I ask to be supported in the trust that all of my basic needs in life are met, that I am connected in healthy ways to my family and tribal consciousness, and that allows me to move with the ebb and flow of life. And so it is."

Yoga

The root chakra is about stability and support. Corresponding asanas would be standing poses that strengthen the legs and ability to ground. Standing balancing poses to regulate this chakra include Warrior I, Warrior II, Tree Pose, and Chair Pose. Seated postures relate to grounding as well. Making sure to stretch the back of the legs is helpful with Standing Forward Bend and Head-to-Knee Pose. Restorative poses such as Reclining Bound Angle Pose, Supported Corpse Pose, and Supported Child's Pose can help us surrender to the gravity and groundedness of this chakra. (For illustrations of yoga poses, see the Appendix on page 146.)

Other Tips

- Eat root vegetables, which will help ground you.
- Take some time to do activities where your bare feet are planted into the earth, soil, or sand.
- Spend some time in nature.
- Make pottery (this will help your sacral plexus chakra, too).
- Stomp your feet to connect with the earth or ground (even if you're in a building).
- Chant the mantra sound for this chakra: "LAM."

THE SACRAL PLEXUS CHAKRA

The sacral plexus chakra is all about connecting with your emotions, creative expression, sexuality, and abundance in healthy ways. The following meditations, crystal techniques, essential oil applications, and yoga postures will help you connect with what you may be holding in this chakra, and most importantly, will initiate connection with this energy vortex within you, so you may open into the wisdom it holds.

Meditations

Here's an easy, tried-and-true meditation and visualization to connect with your sacral plexus chakra:

1. While sitting or lying comfortably, take three slow, deep breaths. Each time you inhale, imagine the breath energizing the area two inches below your navel. Each time you exhale, release anything you may be holding in that area (any fears, pain, or even expectations of how you're supposed to feel while doing this meditation). Holding your hands over your heart as you meditate on each chakra may help you more quickly connect to the chakra you're concentrating on. You may want to have one hand over the heart chakra, and the other hand over your sacral plexus chakra.

2. "Wake up" the connection with this chakra by gently tapping two inches below the navel, or by using your first two fingers to gently massage the area in a small, circular motion.

3. With each following breath, inhaling and exhaling through the nose, continue directing your breath to your sacral plexus chakra. Imagine an orange sphere of light in that area, pulsing and growing larger. Those who identify most with male energy should whirl the sphere counterclockwise, and those who identify most with female energy should whirl the sphere clockwise.

4. As you drop deeper and deeper into a calmer state, ask your sacral plexus chakra what it needs right now. Allow yourself a few more breaths to see if you receive any feedback. It might come in the form of a word, sound, song, image, color, feeling, or intuition. Then act on the feedback you get. If you don't have any yet, not to worry! It will come as you continue practicing.

5. If you don't receive any of the intuitive hints listed previously, but instead feel an awareness in that area, similar to a pulsing or a gentle opening and expansion, you are connecting with your sacral plexus chakra!

6. At the end of your meditation, take three slow, deep breaths, directing the energy of your inhale into the soles of your feet, to ground yourself. Gently open your eyes.

7. *Caution when doing this meditation/visualization:* Because this practice takes some time to cultivate, be patient with yourself. If you find that a belly ache is forming in your lower abdomen, you are pushing yourself too hard. It's time to take a break and revisit when you're more rejuvenated. Also, as you perform your meditation, understand that even seasoned meditation practitioners get what's aptly termed monkey mind, where other thoughts begin to enter your mind and may momentarily distract you. Just take this as a chance to observe the thought without judgment, let it pass through, and gently bring yourself back to center.

Crystals

Carnelian, amber, moonstone, coral, orange tourmaline, and sunstone are the crystals that resonate with the sacral plexus chakra. (For images of these crystals, see the Appendix on page 158.)

To use crystals to connect with your sacral plexus chakra, make sure that they are first cleansed from the energies of others who may have handled them before you, and that your intention for how they will be used is set. You can clean your crystals by:

- Smudging with white sage. Simply light the tip of a white sage bundle until it begins to smoke, blow out the flame, and hold your crystal in the rising smoke for a few seconds, setting the intention that you'll be using the crystal to help you connect with your sacral plexus chakra. This is my favorite method, because after your cleanse your crystal, you can also cleanse your body by directing the smoke toward your chakras (and the rest of your body) with your free hand.

- Laying them out overnight under the moonlight to soak up the moonbeams.

- Running water over them or soaking them in salt water. When cleaning with water, use caution. Any stones that rate low on the Mohs hardness scale (a scale that helps identify mineral specimens and compares the resistance to being scratched) may get damaged or dissolve as a result.

Now that you've cleansed and charged them, you can work with them in a few ways:

- Get into a comfortable seated or lying down position. Hold the crystal in your left hand—the receiving hand—so you can receive the healing energy from the crystal. Notice what you pick up from the crystal. Does it feel like a throbbing in your hand? Like static prickles? Or just a simple awareness of its energy? If you don't feel any of these things, that's okay. Sometimes it takes a while to create an awareness with a stone's energy. Ask the crystal to help you connect with the wisdom of your sacral plexus chakra. Allow your mind and heart to open to receive any feedback, in the way of images, colors, sounds, words, memories, emotions, or other impressions that may flow through. Keep in mind that working with crystals can take some getting used to. So, if your sacral plexus chakra doesn't open into an epiphany right on the spot (which is unlikely on a first try, but anything is possible!), understand that you are still one step closer to being more connected with it. Be compassionate with yourself. Know that it is on its way.

- While lying down, place your selected sacral plexus chakra crystal two inches below your navel. Take three slow and deep breaths. Allow yourself to drink in the energy of the crystal. As with the preceding holding technique, you may feel the energy at this chakra pulse, like a gentle heartbeat. You may feel a slight static energy. Or you may have an awareness that the crystal's energy is interacting with your energy. If you don't feel any of these things, that's okay. You may want to say the affirmation in the last paragraph of the Essential Oils section to more intentionally connect with your sacral plexus chakra.

Essential Oils

Ylang ylang, lemon, patchouli, rosewood, and sandalwood are the essential oils that correspond with the sacral plexus chakra.

To use a single oil (or a blend of oils) to help you connect with this chakra, add 5 or 6 drops maximum per oil to a dime-size portion of carrier oil (such as jojoba oil). Apply with a cotton ball to the sacral plexus chakra, located two inches below the navel, to anoint yourself.

Or, you can put the mixture in your hands and rub your hands together. Through friction, you will release the scent and energy of the oils. Open your palms to release the fragrance. Deeply inhale the scent. You may also want to lay your hands over the chakra area.

Whether you choose to anoint your sacral plexus chakra, or activate the properties of the oils by rubbing them between your palms, take the time to intentionally create a connection with your sacral plexus chakra.

While you anoint yourself, or take in the scent of the activated oils in your palms, say something like, "I now intend to create a connection with my sacral plexus chakra. May I be in touch with my emotions in healthy ways, creatively express myself to the world, and connect easily to my pleasure, as well as the emotional aspects of my sexuality, in ways that sustain me. I release all fear that keeps me from being in touch with my emotions, creativity, abundance, and sexuality. I ask to be supported in the harmony of my emotions and clairsentience, so that I may be at peace with how I feel. And so it is."

Yoga

The sacral plexus chakra is about sweetness and creativity, but is also the seat of our physical strength. Corresponding poses would be anything that fires up our core muscles, such as four limbed staff posture and all the warrior poses. Creativity and the water element may be nurtured through flowing movement and breath, promoting flexibility in the lower spine—Child's Pose, Happy Baby Pose, and Downward Facing Dog are excellent poses for this. Other poses can help open the hip and groin, such as Cow Face Pose, Bound Angle Pose, Open Angel Pose, and the forward bending of the legs in the first stage of Pigeon Pose. (For illustrations of yoga poses, see the Appendix on page 146.)

Other Tips

- Dance—especially belly dancing, Latin dances such as salsa, and other dances that move the hip area.

- Practice hula-hooping.

- Learn tantra to get in touch with your sexuality on a more conscious level.

- Try journaling, writing, painting, or another form of creative expression to help channel your emotions.

- Learn how to express your emotions in healthy ways.

- Include play in your daily life to cultivate flexibility in learning how to experience pleasure and joy.

- Chant the mantra sound corresponding to this chakra: "VAM."

THE SOLAR PLEXUS CHAKRA

The solar plexus chakra is all about standing in your power, getting in touch with your inner warrior fire, and self-esteem. The following meditations, crystal techniques, essential oil applications, and yoga postures will help you connect with what you may be holding in this chakra, and, most importantly, initiate connection with this energy vortex within you, so you may open into the wisdom it holds.

Meditations

Here's an easy, tried-and-true meditation and visualization to connect with your solar plexus chakra:

1. While sitting or lying comfortably, take three slow, deep breaths. Each time you breathe in, imagine the breath energizing the area above your navel. Each time you exhale, release anything you may be holding in that area—any fears, pain, or even expectations of how you're supposed to feel while doing this meditation. Personally, I find that holding my hands over my heart as I meditate on each chakra helps me more quickly connect to the chakra I'm concentrating on. You may want to place one hand over your heart chakra, and the other hand over your solar plexus chakra.

2. "Wake up" the connection with this chakra by gently tapping two inches above the navel, or by gently massaging the area in a small, circular motion with your first two fingers.

3. With each following breath, inhaling and exhaling through the nose, continue directing your breath to your solar plexus chakra. Imagine a yellow sphere of light in that area, pulsing and growing larger. Those who identify most with male energy should whirl the sphere clockwise, and those who identify most with female energy should whirl the sphere counterclockwise.

4. As you drop deeper and deeper into a calmer state, ask your solar plexus chakra what it needs right now. Allow yourself a few more breaths to see if you receive any feedback. It could be in the form of a word, sound, song, image, color, feeling, or intuition. Then act on the feedback you get. If you don't have any yet, not to worry! It will come as you continue practicing.

5. If you don't receive any of the intuitive hints listed previously, but instead feel an awareness in that area, similar to a pulsing or a gentle ache that feels like it's expanding and strengthening, you are connecting with your solar plexus chakra!

6. At the end of your meditation, take three slow, deep breaths, directing the energy of your inhale into the soles of your feet, to ground yourself. Gently open your eyes.

7. *Caution when doing this meditation/visualization:* Because this practice takes some time to cultivate, be patient with yourself. If you find yourself beginning to feel a stomach ache, you are pushing yourself too hard. It's time to take a break and revisit when you're more rejuvenated. Also, as you perform your meditation, understand that even seasoned meditation practitioners get what's aptly termed monkey mind, where other thoughts begin to enter your mind and may momentarily distract you. Just take this as a chance to observe the thought without judgment, let it pass through, and gently bring yourself back to center.

Crystals

Yellow citrine, amber, yellow topaz, yellow tiger's eye, yellow agate, and rutilated quartz are the crystals that resonate with the solar plexus chakra. (For images of these crystals, see the Appendix on page 158.)

To use crystals to connect with your solar plexus chakra, make sure that they are first cleansed from the energies of others who may have handled them before you, and that your intention for how they will be used is set. You can clean your crystals by:

- Smudging with white sage. Simply light the tip of a white sage bundle until it begins to smoke, blow out the flame, and hold your crystal in the rising smoke for a few seconds, setting the intention that you'll be using the crystal to help you connect with your solar plexus chakra. This is my favorite method, because after your cleanse your crystal, you can also cleanse your body by directing the smoke toward your chakras (and the rest of your body) with your free hand.

- Laying them out overnight under the moonlight to soak up the moonbeams.

- Running water over them or soaking them in salt water. When cleaning with water, use caution. Any stones that rate low on the Mohs hardness scale (a scale that helps identify mineral specimens and compares the resistance to being scratched) may get damaged or dissolve as a result.

Now that you've cleansed and charged your crystals, you can work with them in a few ways:

- Get into a comfortable seated or lying down position. Hold your crystal in your left hand—the receiving hand—so you can receive the healing energy from the crystal. Notice what you pick up from the crystal. Does it feel like a throbbing in your hand? Like static prickles? Or just a simple awareness of its energy? If you don't feel any of these things, that's okay. Sometimes it takes a while to create an awareness with a stone's energy. Ask the crystal to help you connect with the wisdom of your solar plexus chakra. Allow your mind and heart to open to receive any feedback, in the way of images, colors, sounds, words, memories, emotions, or other impressions that may flow through. Keep in mind that working with crystals can take some getting used to. So, if your solar plexus chakra doesn't open into an epiphany right on the spot (which is unlikely on a first try, but anything is possible!), understand that you are still one step closer to being more connected with it. Be compassionate with yourself. Know that it is on its way.

- While lying down, place your selected solar plexus chakra crystal two inches above your navel. Take three slow and deep breaths. Allow yourself to drink in the energy of the crystal. As with the preceding holding technique, you may feel the energy at the chakra area, like a gentle heartbeat. You may feel a slight static energy. Or you may have an awareness that the crystal's energy is interacting with your energy. If you don't feel any of these things, that's okay. You may want to say the affirmation listed in the last paragraph of the Essential Oils section to more intentionally connect with your solar plexus chakra.

Essential Oils

Lemon, lavender, Roman chamomile, rosewood, and rosemary are the essential oils that correspond with the solar plexus chakra.

To use a single oil (or a blend of oils) to help you connect with this chakra, add 5 or 6 drops maximum per oil to a dime-size portion of carrier oil (such as jojoba oil). Apply with a cotton ball to the solar plexus chakra, two inches above your navel, to anoint yourself.

Alternately, you can put the mixture in your hands and rub your hands together. Through the friction, you will release the scent and energy of the oils. Open your palms to release the fragrance, and deeply inhale the scent. You may also want to lay your palms over your solar plexus chakra.

Whether you choose to anoint your solar plexus chakra, or activate the properties of the oils by rubbing them between your palms, take the time to intentionally create a connection with your solar plexus chakra. Say something like, "I now intend to create a connection with my solar plexus chakra. May I understand my self-worth and personal power. I release all fear that keeps me from being in touch with my soul's life purpose. I ask to be supported in all ways so that I may be in touch with my inner warrior, feel whole and centered in who I am, and trust myself to stand confidently. And so it is."

Yoga

The solar plexus chakra is the center of personal power and confidence, so any pose that moves with a lot of energy, makes you feel very strong, fans the flame of your inner fire, or asks that your middle spine be flexible would be good here. Try Cat Pose, Cow Pose, Sun Salutation, Boat Pose, or Half Boat Pose. (For illustrations of yoga poses, see the Appendix on page 146.) Leg lifts are also very effective, or you can try breathing exercises like Breath of Fire or Bellows Breath.

A note about Breath of Fire and Bellows Breath: These breathing exercises can fire up the metabolism and generate a lot of energy, so you should avoid doing these too close to bedtime. Breath of Fire is performed through the nose, with the mouth closed. The focus is on exhaling—the breath is forced out quickly by drawing the abdomen in and up sharply. This causes the air to be expelled rapidly from the lungs, and inhaling happens automatically before the next forced exhale. The Bellows Breath focuses equally on inhaling and exhaling through the nose while the mouth is closed. Here, the origination of action comes from the navel pumping in for the exhale *and* out for the inhale. This practice is not performed as rapidly as Breath of Fire, but instead is performed in a rhythmic and full manner.

Other Tips

- Wear yellow clothing.
- Chant the sound "RA," which opens up the solar plexus chakra.
- Take martial arts (internal or external), which helps strengthen personal power.
- Create healthy energy boundaries with those in your life to strengthen your inner power. A simple way to create an energy boundary is by surrounding yourself in an egg of white light, especially if you're about to enter a stressful situation, such as a talk with a toxic coworker, or, if you experience social anxiety, before entering a large room full of people.
- Try things outside your comfort zone. Doing so helps you build confidence in your own resilience.

THE HEART CHAKRA

The heart chakra is all about being connected with yourself, as well as cultivating joy, self-love, and compassion. The following meditations, crystal techniques, essential oil applications, and yoga postures will help you connect with what you may be holding in this chakra. Most importantly, they should help you initiate connection with this energy vortex within you, so you may open into the wisdom it holds.

Meditations

Here's an easy, tried-and-true meditation and visualization to connect with your heart chakra:

1. While sitting or lying down comfortably, take three slow, deep breaths. Each time you inhale, imagine the breath energizing the center of your chest. Each time you exhale, release anything you may be holding in that area—any fears, pain, or even expectations around how you're supposed to feel while doing this meditation. Holding your hands over your heart as you meditate on each chakra may help you more quickly connect to the chakra you're concentrating on—especially the heart chakra!

2. "Wake up" the connection with this chakra by gently tapping the center of the chest, or by gently massaging the area in a small, circular motion with your first two fingers.

3. With each following breath, inhaling and exhaling through the nose, continue directing your breath to your heart chakra. Imagine a green sphere of light in that area, pulsing and growing larger. Those who identify most with male energy should whirl the sphere counterclockwise, and those who identify most with female energy should whirl the sphere clockwise.

4. As you drop deeper and deeper into a calmer state, ask your heart chakra what it needs right now. Allow yourself a few more breaths to see if you receive any feedback. It could be in the form of a word, sound, song, image, color, feeling, or intuition. Then act on the feedback you get. If you don't get any immediate feedback, not to worry! It will come as you continue practicing.

5. If you don't receive any of the intuitive hints listed previously, you may instead feel an awareness in that area, similar to an expansion in your chest, or a feeling like the energy at the center your chest is rising slightly upward. If so, you are connecting with your heart chakra!

6. At the end of your meditation, take three slow, deep breaths, directing the energy of your inhales into the soles of your feet, grounding yourself. Gently open your eyes.

7. *Caution when doing this meditation/visualization:* Because this practice takes some time to cultivate, be patient with yourself. If you find that your heart rate is elevating in a way that is uncomfortable, you are pushing yourself too hard. It's time to take a break and revisit when you're more rejuvenated. Also, as you perform your meditation, understand that even seasoned meditation practitioners get what's aptly termed monkey mind, where other thoughts begin to enter your mind and may momentarily distract you. Just take this as a chance to observe the thought without judgment, let it pass through, and gently bring yourself back to center.

Crystals

Rose quartz, emerald, green tourmaline, jade, green calcite, green kyanite, and peridot are the crystals that resonate with the heart chakra. (For images of these crystals, see the Appendix on page 158.)

To use crystals to connect with your heart chakra, make sure that they are first cleansed from the energies of others who may have handled them before you, and that your intention for how they will be used is set. You can clean your crystals by:

- Smudging with white sage. Simply light the tip of a white sage bundle until it begins to smoke, blow out the flame, and hold your crystal in the rising smoke for a few seconds, setting the intention that you'll be using the crystal to help you connect with your heart chakra. This is my favorite method, because after your cleanse your crystal, you can also cleanse your body by directing the smoke toward your chakras (and the rest of your body) with your free hand.

- Laying them out overnight under the moonlight to soak up the moonbeams.

- Running water over them or soaking them in salt water. When cleaning with water, use caution. Any stones that rate low on the Mohs hardness scale (a scale that helps identify mineral specimens and compares the resistance to being scratched) may get damaged or dissolve as a result.

Now that you've cleansed and charged your crystals, you can work with them in a few ways:

- Get into a comfortable seated or lying down position. Hold the crystal in your left hand—the receiving hand—so you can receive the healing energy from the crystal. Notice what you pick up from the crystal. Does it feel like a throbbing in your hand? Like static prickles? Or just a simple awareness of its energy? If you don't feel any of these things, that's okay. Sometimes it takes a while to create an awareness with a stone's energy. Ask the crystal to help you connect with the wisdom of your heart chakra. Allow your mind and heart to open to feedback in the way of images, colors, sounds, words, memories, emotions, or other impressions that may flow through. Keep in mind that working with crystals can take some getting used to. So, if your heart chakra doesn't open into an epiphany right on the spot (which is unlikely on a first try, but anything is possible!), understand that you are still one step closer to being more connected with it. Be compassionate with yourself. Know that it is on its way.

- While lying down, place your selected heart chakra crystal at the center of your chest. Take three slow and deep breaths. Allow yourself to drink in the crystal's energy. As with the preceding holding technique, you may feel the energy expand within your heart. You may feel a slight static energy. Or you may have an awareness that the crystal's energy is interacting with your energy. If you don't feel any of these things, that's okay. You may want to say the affirmation listed in the last paragraph of the Essential Oils section to more intentionally connect with your heart chakra.

Essential Oils

Rose, geranium, neroli, palmarosa, bergamot, lavender, melissa/lemon balm, and ylang ylang are the essential oils that correspond with the heart chakra.

To use a single oil (or a blend of oils) to help you connect with this chakra, add 5 or 6 drops maximum per oil to a dime-size portion of carrier oil (such as jojoba oil). Apply with a cotton ball to the heart chakra, at the center of your chest, to anoint yourself.

Or, you can put the mixture in your hands, and rub your hands together. Through the friction, you will release the scent and energy of the oils. Open your palms to release the fragrance, and deeply inhale the scent. You may also want to simply lay your hands on your heart, with the activated oils.

Whether you choose to anoint your heart chakra or activate the properties of the oils by rubbing them between your palms, take the time to intentionally create a connection with your heart chakra. Say something like, "I now intend to create a connection with my heart chakra. May I fully and completely connect with myself in loving and compassionate ways, and extend that outward to those around me. I release all fear that keeps me from receiving and giving love. I ask to be supported in elevating the vibration of my heart to one of joy. May I love and accept all of myself, including my flaws. And so it is."

Yoga

The heart chakra is the heart center and seat of our soul. Using yoga to open this area of our bodies could be done with upper backbends, such as in Camel Pose, and chest openers, such as a Seated Spinal Twist. Eagle Pose is good for the backside of this chakra (the arm positioning spreads the shoulder blades wide). In addition, arm balances are good to help your heart, dreams, and wishes take flight. (For illustrations of yoga poses, see the Appendix on page 146.)

Other Tips

- Buy yourself a bouquet of roses. Roses resonate at the heart chakra.

- Make yourself rosebud tea. These tiny rosebuds, which you can buy at herb shops, specialty tea shops, and at many health food stores and Asian markets, are actually a Chinese medicinal herb called *mei gui hua*. By steeping a few buds in a large mug of hot water for a few minutes, you can create a love ritual for yourself and ingest the love of the roses.

- Practice forgiveness—of yourself and others.

- Chant to the mantra sound of "YUM."

- Be open with genuine love and affection for those you truly love.

THE THROAT CHAKRA

The throat chakra is all about speaking your truth, effectively communicating your needs, and expressing yourself. The following meditations, crystal techniques, essential oil applications, and yoga postures will help you connect with what you may be holding in this chakra, and, most importantly, initiate connection with this energy vortex within you, so that you may open into the wisdom it holds.

Meditations

Here's an easy, tried-and-true meditation and visualization to connect with your throat chakra:

1. While sitting or lying down comfortably, take three slow, deep breaths. Each time you breathe in, imagine the breath energizing the notch at the front of your throat. Each time you exhale, release anything you may be holding in that area—any fears, pain, or even expectations of how you're supposed to feel while doing this meditation. Personally, I find that holding my hands over my heart as I meditate on each chakra helps me connect to the chakra I'm concentrating on more quickly. You may want to place one hand on your heart chakra and the other hand at your throat.

2. "Wake up" the connection with this chakra by gently tapping at the bone in front of the notch at the front of your throat, or by gently massaging the area in a small, circular motion with your first two fingers.

3. With each following breath, inhaling and exhaling through the nose, continue directing your breath to your throat chakra. Imagine that there is a light blue sphere of light in that area, pulsing and growing larger. Those who identify most with male energy should whirl the sphere clockwise, and those who identify most with female energy should whirl the sphere counterclockwise.

4. As you drop deeper and deeper into a calmer state, ask your throat chakra what it needs right now. Allow yourself a few more breaths to see if you receive any feedback. It could be in the form of a word, sound, song, image, color, feeling, or intuition. Then act on the feedback you get. If you don't get any immediate feedback, not to worry! It will come as you continue practicing.

5. If instead of the intuitive hints listed previously, you feel an awareness similar to a sensation of opening, widening, or expansion in your throat area, you are connecting with your throat chakra!

6. At the end of your meditation, take three slow, deep breaths, directing the energy of your inhale into the soles of your feet, grounding yourself. Gently open your eyes.

7. *Caution when doing this meditation/visualization:* Because this practice takes some time to cultivate, be patient with yourself. If you notice that you're feeling pain in your neck, you are pushing yourself too hard. It's time to take a break and revisit when you're more rejuvenated. Also, as you perform your meditation, understand that even seasoned meditation practitioners get what's aptly termed monkey mind, where other thoughts begin to enter your mind and may momentarily distract you. Just take this as a chance to observe the thought without judgment, let it pass through, and gently bring yourself back to center.

Crystals

Turquoise, blue kyanite, aquamarine, celestite, iolite, sodalite, and lapis lazuli are the crystals that resonate with the throat chakra. (For images of these crystals, see the Appendix on page 158.)

To use crystals to connect with your throat chakra, make sure that they are first cleansed from the energies of others who may have handled them before you, and that your intention for how they will be used is set. You can clean your crystals by:

- Smudging with white sage. Simply light the tip of a white sage bundle until it begins to smoke, blow out the flame, and hold your crystal in the rising smoke for a few seconds, setting the intention that you'll be using the crystal to help you connect with your throat chakra. This is my favorite method, because after your cleanse your crystal, you can also cleanse your body by directing the smoke toward your chakras (and the rest of your body) with your free hand.

- Laying them out overnight under the moonlight to soak up he moonbeams.

- Running water over them or soaking them in salt water. When cleaning with water, use caution. Any stones that rate low on the Mohs hardness scale (a scale that helps identify mineral specimens and compares the resistance to being scratched) may get damaged or dissolve as a result.

Now that you've cleansed and charged your crystals, you can work with them in a few ways:

- Get into a comfortable seated or lying down position. Hold your chosen crystal in your left hand—the receiving hand—so you can receive the healing energy from the crystal. Notice what you pick up from the crystal. Does it feel like a throbbing in your hand? Like static prickles? Or just a simple awareness of its energy? If you don't feel any of these things, that's okay. Sometimes it takes a while to create an awareness with a stone's energy. Ask the crystal to help you connect with the wisdom of your throat chakra. Allow your mind and heart to open to feedback in the way of images, colors, sounds, words, memories, emotions, or other impressions that may flow through. Keep in mind that working with crystals can take some getting used to. So, if your throat chakra doesn't open into an epiphany right on the spot (which is unlikely on a first try, but anything is possible!), understand that you are still one step closer to being more connected with it. Be compassionate with yourself. Know that it is on its way.

- While lying down, place your selected throat chakra crystal at the notch at the base of your front neck. Take three slow and deep breaths. Allow yourself to drink in the energy of the crystal. As with the preceding holding technique, you may feel the energy at your neck pulse, like a gentle heartbeat. You may feel a slight static energy. Or you may have an awareness that the crystal's energy is interacting with your energy. If you don't feel any of these things, that's okay. You may want to say the affirmation listed in the last paragraph of the Essential Oils section to more intentionally connect with your throat chakra.

Essential Oils

Lavender, rosemary, frankincense, German chamomile, and hyssop are the essential oils that correspond with the throat chakra.

To use a single oil (or blend of oils) to help you connect with this chakra, add 5 or 6 drops maximum per oil to a dime-size portion of carrier oil (such as jojoba oil). Apply with a cotton ball to the throat chakra, located at the notch at the base of the throat, to anoint yourself.

Alternately, put the mixture in your hands and rub them together. Through friction, you will release the scent and energy of the oils. Open your palms to release the fragrance. Then, deeply inhale the scent.

Whether you choose to anoint your throat chakra or activate the properties of the oils by rubbing them between your palms, take the time to intentionally create a connection with your throat chakra. Say something like, "I now intend to create a connection with my throat chakra. May I be in touch with my will to live and may I speak my truth in this world authentically, creatively, and easily. I release all fear that keeps me from listening to my inner voice. I ask to be supported in all forms of personal expression, so I may communicate my needs effortlessly, and trust that I will be heard. And so it is."

Yoga

The throat chakra is about speaking your truth, so neck flexibility helps with fluency here. Most poses have a specific focal point (otherwise known as drishti) for the eyes—the head follows the eyes, and the body follows the head. The neck has to be open for the head to turn. Great yoga poses for this are Warrior II, Camel Pose, Bridge Pose, Triangle Pose, Extended Side Angle, Shoulderstand, and Plow Pose. Most twisting postures can aid the throat chakra as well. (For illustrations of yoga poses, see the Appendix on page 146.)

Other Tips

- Say what you mean, and mean what you say.
- Practice chanting, singing, reading aloud, or humming.
- Chant the mantra sound for this chakra: "HUM."
- Wear the color light blue.
- Drink teas that soothe the throat, such as peppermint, slippery elm, and spearmint.

THE THIRD EYE CHAKRA

The third eye chakra is all about trusting your intuition and inner vision. The following meditations, crystal techniques, essential oil applications, and yoga postures will help you connect with what you may be holding in this chakra, and, most importantly, initiate connection with this energy vortex within you, so you may open into the wisdom it holds.

To increase your connection with your third eye chakra, make sure you drink unfluoridated water. Fluoride calcifies the pineal gland, which is related to the third eye. An effective water purification system is helpful for this purpose.

Meditations

Here's an easy, tried-and-true meditation and visualization to connect with your third eye chakra:

1. While sitting or lying down comfortably, take three slow, deep breaths. Each time you breathe in, imagine the breath energizing the area between your brows. Each time you exhale, release anything you may be holding in that area (any fears, pain, or even expectations of how you're supposed to feel while doing this meditation). Personally, I find that holding my hands over my heart as I meditate on each chakra helps me more quickly connect to the chakra I'm concentrating on. Or, you can try placing one hand over your heart chakra and your other hand over the area between your eyebrows.

2. "Wake up" the connection with this chakra by gently tapping between your eyebrows, or by gently massaging the area in a small, circular motion with your first two fingers.

3. With each following breath, inhaling and exhaling through the nose, continue directing your breath to your third eye chakra. Imagine that there is an indigo sphere of light in that area, pulsing and growing larger. Those who identify most with male energy should whirl the sphere counterclockwise, and those who identify most with female energy should whirl the sphere clockwise.

4. As you drop deeper and deeper into a calmer state, ask your third eye chakra what it needs right now. Allow yourself a few more breaths to see if you receive any feedback. It could be in the form of a word, sound, song, image, color, feeling, or intuition. Then act on the feedback you get. If you don't have any yet, not to worry! It will come as you continue practicing.

5. If, instead of receiving one of the intuitive hints listed previously, you instead feel an awareness, similar to a pulsing or a gentle ache that feels like a thumb is being pressed against that area of your head, you are connecting with your third eye chakra!

6. At the end of your meditation, take three slow, deep breaths directing the energy of your inhale into the soles of your feet, to ground yourself. Gently open your eyes.

7. *Caution when doing this meditation/visualization:* Because this practice takes some time to cultivate, be patient with yourself. If you find that you're forming a frontal headache, you are pushing yourself too hard. It's time to take a break and revisit when you're more rejuvenated. Also, as you perform your meditation, understand that even seasoned meditation practitioners get what's aptly termed monkey mind, where other thoughts begin to enter your mind and may momentarily distract you. Just take this as a chance to observe the thought without judgment, let it pass through, and gently bring yourself back to center.

Crystals

Lapis lazuli, amethyst, fluorite, lepidolite, sugilite, tanzanite, clear quartz, star sapphire, and kyanite are the crystals that resonate with the third eye chakra. (For images of these crystals, see the Appendix on page 158.)

To use crystals to connect with your third eye chakra, make sure that they are first cleansed from the energies of others who may have handled them before you, and that your intention for how they will be used is set. You can clean your crystals by:

- Smudging with white sage. Simply light the tip of a white sage bundle until it begins to smoke, blow out the flame, and hold your crystal in the rising smoke for a few seconds, setting the intention that you'll be using the crystal to help you connect with your third eye chakra. This is my favorite method, because after your cleanse your crystal, you can also cleanse your body by directing the smoke toward your chakras (and the rest of your body) with your free hand.

- Laying them out overnight under the moonlight to soak up the moonbeams.

- Running water over them or soaking them in salt water. When cleaning with water, use caution. Any stones that rate low on the Mohs hardness scale (a scale that helps identify mineral specimens and compares the resistance to being scratched) may get damaged or dissolve as a result.

Now that you've cleansed and charged them, you can work with them in a few ways:

- Get into a comfortable seated or lying down position. Hold the crystal in your left hand—the receiving hand—so you can receive the healing energy from the crystal. Notice what you pick up from the crystal. Does it feel like a throbbing in your hand? Like static prickles? Or just a simple awareness of its energy? If you don't feel any of these things, that's okay. Sometimes it takes a while to create an awareness with a stone's energy. Ask it to help you connect with the wisdom of your third eye chakra. Allow your mind and heart to open to receive any feedback, in the way of images, colors, sounds, words, memories, emotions, or other impressions that may flow through. Keep in mind that working with crystals can take some getting used to. So, if your third eye chakra doesn't open into an epiphany right on the spot (which is unlikely on a first try, but anything is possible!), understand that you are one step closer to being more connected with it, be compassionate with yourself. Know that it is on its way.

- While lying down, place your selected third eye chakra crystal between your eyebrows. Take three slow and deep breaths, and allow yourself to drink in the energy of the crystal. As with the preceding holding technique, you may feel the energy pulsing between your brows, like a gentle heartbeat. You may feel a slight static energy. Or you may have an awareness that the crystal's energy is interacting with your energy. If you don't feel any of these things, that's okay. You may want to say the affirmation listed in the last paragraph of the Essential Oils section to more intentionally connect with your third eye chakra.

Essential Oils

Lavender, frankincense, and sandalwood are the essential oils that correspond with the third eye chakra.

To use a single oil (or a blend of oils) to help you connect with this chakra, add 5 or 6 drops maximum per oil to a dime-size portion of carrier oil (such as jojoba oil). Apply with a cotton ball to the third eye chakra, at the area between your brows, to anoint yourself.

Alternately, you can put the mixture in your hands and rub them together. Through the friction, you will release the scent and energy of the oils. Open your palms to release the fragrance. Deeply inhale the scent.

Whether you choose to anoint your third eye chakra, or activate the properties of the oils by rubbing them between your palms, take the time to intentionally create a connection with your third eye chakra. Say something like, "I now intend to create a connection with my third eye chakra. I now release all fear that keeps me from trusting my intuition. May I trust and follow it, and see past what is physically in front of me, so that I may see all possibilities with ease. May I effortlessly integrate my inner vision into all aspects of my life, and allow myself to connect with the emotional intelligence of my third eye. And so it is."

Yoga

For the third eye chakra, the focus is to see things from all perspectives—all poses right-side up, upside down, twisted, or eyes closed. Try wearing a blindfold during a set of poses to experience *pratyahara*, or the drawing inward of the senses. This helps direct your vision more deeply inside yourself, which can aid this chakra. In addition, doing supported Forward Bends using an extra bolster or blanket helps press upon and stimulate this chakra. (For illustrations of yoga poses, see the Appendix on page 146.)

Other Tips

- When you receive an intuitive hint, act on it. It will strengthen your intuition.
- Chant the mantra sound: "SHAM."
- Set the intention that you wish to connect with your inner wisdom.
- Add dark blue and indigo colors to your wardrobe.
- Eat foods such as black currants, blueberries, blackberries, eggplant, prunes, beets, and rainbow chard.
- Remove fluoride from your diet using a water purifying system because fluoride calcifies the pineal gland, which is directly linked to the third eye chakra.

THE CROWN CHAKRA

The crown chakra is all about becoming more connected with our Inner Divine, as well as our connection to the Divine. The following meditations, crystal techniques, essential oil applications, and yoga postures will help you connect with what you may be holding in this chakra. Most importantly, these techniques will help you initiate connection with this energy vortex within you so you may open into the wisdom it holds.

Meditation

Here's an easy, tried-and-true meditation and visualization to connect with your crown chakra:

1. While sitting or lying down comfortably, take three slow, deep breaths. Each time you breathe in, imagine the breath energizing the top center of your head. Each time you exhale, release anything you may be holding in that area (any fears, pain, or even expectations of how you're supposed to feel while doing this meditation). Personally, I find that holding my hands over my heart as I meditate on each chakra helps me more quickly connect to the chakra I'm concentrating on. Another option might be to place one hand over your heart chakra and your other hand over the top of your head.

2. "Wake up" the connection with this chakra by gently tapping at the top of the center of the head, or by gently massaging the area in a small, circular motion with your first two fingers.

3. With each following breath, inhaling and exhaling through the nose, continue directing your breath to your crown chakra. Imagine that there is a purple (or white or gold) sphere of light in that area, pulsing and growing larger. Those who identify most with male energy should whirl the sphere clockwise, and those who identify most with female energy should whirl the sphere counterclockwise.

4. As you drop deeper and deeper into a calmer state, ask your crown chakra what it needs right now. Allow yourself a few more breaths to see if you receive any feedback. It could be in the form of a word, sound, song, image, color, feeling, or intuition. Then act on the feedback you get. If you don't have any yet, don't worry! It will come as you continue practicing.

5. If you don't receive any of the intuitive hints listed previously, but instead feel an awareness, similar to a pulsing or a gentle ache that feels like it's connecting with the space directly above your head (or shooting much farther up above you), you are connecting with your crown chakra!

6. At the end of your meditation, take three slow, deep breaths, directing the energy of your inhale into the soles of your feet, to ground yourself. Gently open your eyes.

7. *Caution when doing this meditation/visualization*: Because this practice takes some time to cultivate, be patient with yourself. If you find yourself starting to experience a vertex headache, or a headache located at the top of your head, you are pushing yourself too hard. It's time to take a break and revisit when you're more rejuvenated. Also, as you perform your meditation, understand that even seasoned meditation practitioners get what's aptly termed monkey mind, where other thoughts begin to enter your mind and may momentarily distract you. Just take this as a chance to observe the thought without judgment, let it pass through, and gently bring yourself back to center.

Crystals

Amethyst, clear quartz, Herkimer diamond, labradorite, moonstone, selenite, phenacite, kunzite, apophyllite, and white topaz are the crystals that resonate with the crown chakra. (For images of these crystals, see the Appendix on page 158.)

To use crystals to connect with your crown chakra, make sure that they are first cleansed from the energies of others who may have handled them before you, and that your intention for how they will be used is set. You can clean your crystals by:

- Smudging with white sage. Simply light the tip of a white sage bundle until it begins to smoke, blow out the flame, and hold your crystal in the rising smoke for a few seconds, setting the intention that you'll be using the crystal to help you connect with your crown chakra. This is my favorite method, because after your cleanse your crystal, you can also cleanse your body by directing the smoke toward your chakras (and the rest of your body) with your free hand.

- Laying them out overnight under the moonlight to soak up the moonbeams.

- Running water over them or soaking them in salt water. When cleaning with water, use caution. Any stones that rate low on the Mohs hardness scale (a scale that helps identify mineral specimens and compares the resistance to being scratched) may get damaged or dissolve as a result.

Now that you've cleansed and charged your crystals, you can work with them in a few ways:

- Get into a comfortable seated or lying down position. Hold your crystal in your left hand—the receiving hand—so you can receive the healing energy from the crystal. Notice what you pick up from the crystal. Does it feel like a throbbing in your hand? Like static prickles? Or just a simple awareness of its energy? If you don't feel any of these things, that's okay. Sometimes it takes a while to create an awareness with a stone's energy. You may ask the crystal to help you connect with the wisdom of your crown chakra. Allow your mind and heart to open to feedback in the way of images, colors, sounds, words, memories, emotions, or other impressions that may flow through. Keep in mind that working with crystals can take some getting used to. So, if your crown chakra doesn't open into an epiphany right on the spot (which is unlikely on a first try, but anything is possible!), understand that you are still one step closer to being more connected with it. Be compassionate with yourself. Know that it is on its way.

- While lying down, place your selected crown chakra crystal at the top center of your head. Take three slow and deep breaths. Allow yourself to drink in the energy of the crystal. As with the preceding holding technique, you may feel the energy at the top of your head pulse, like a gentle heartbeat. You may feel a slight static energy. Or you may have an awareness that the crystal's energy is interacting with your energy. If you don't feel any of these things, that's okay. You may want to say the affirmation listed in the last paragraph of the Essential Oils section to more intentionally connect with your crown chakra.

Essential Oils

Frankincense, peppermint, sandalwood, and lotus are the essential oils that correspond with the crown chakra.

To use a single oil (or a blend of oils) to help you connect with this chakra, add 5 or 6 drops maximum per oil to a dime-size portion of carrier oil (such as jojoba oil). Apply with a cotton ball to the crown chakra, at the top center of the head, to anoint yourself.

Alternately, put the mixture in your hands and rub them together. Through the friction, you will release the scent and energy of the oils. Open your palms to release the fragrance. Deeply inhale the scent.

Whether you choose to anoint your crown chakra or activate the properties of the oils by rubbing them between your palms, take the time to intentionally create a connection with your crown chakra. Say something like, "I now intend to create a connection with my crown chakra. May I understand that I am a reflection of the Divine/Source/Universe/God/dess. I release all fear that keeps me from trusting my path. I ask to be supported in the elevation of my consciousness, so I may live in the knowledge of Unity, and trust that my life is unfolding exactly as it should. And so it is."

Yoga

To cultivate the crown chakra with yoga, headstands are a great way to increase blood flow to the head, which makes you ready to receive information from the Divine. Because headstands are an advanced yoga posture and have a higher risk of injury (Headstand and Shoulderstand, for example, may not be appropriate for beginners or anyone with a neck injury), they should be done with the support and guidance of a trained yoga teacher. Meditation is also recommended as a yogic practice to aid in balancing this chakra. (For illustrations of yoga poses, see the Appendix on page 146.)

Other Tips

- Practice gratitude.
- Cultivate a meditative practice.
- Chant the mantra sound of "OM."
- Wear the color purple or white.
- Set an intention that you are in touch with your crown chakra, the Divine within yourself, and the Divine/Source/Universe/God/dess.

HEALING MULTIPLE CHAKRAS

Because everything is connected, so too are our chakra systems. For instance, one chakra's imbalance can create a reverberating effect on the others.

For example, one of my patients, Ms. M, initially came into my office to treat her cervical dysplasia. During her childhood and into adulthood, her parents were mentally and emotionally unavailable. Her father was especially distant. He spoke to her in ways that made her feel like she was only worthy if she was attractive, but also made her feel ashamed of her growing body during adolescence. In an effort to gain her father's attention and approval, as well as to escape her pain, she developed an eating disorder to control her weight, began abusing substances, and started engaging in other unhealthy behaviors.

Ms. M's experience of her root chakra disharmony—an experience that began with not feeling accepted for who she was by her family— eventually grew to affect her power center, her solar plexus chakra. She felt challenged in her self-worth and self-confidence, which she tried to control with her bulimia.

Not coincidentally, she had grown to mistrust her inner wisdom, her third eye chakra, and unknowingly perpetuated the silencing of her throat chakra that she'd felt growing up. Strong feelings of shame resided in her sacral plexus chakra. She was looking to heal her relationship to herself, her emotions, and her body, and to engage in healthier habits. Although numerous chakras were in need of balancing and her healing journey sometimes left her feeling shaken and vulnerable, her dedication to her personal growth never wavered.

Her focus on self-love has helped her heal and grow exponentially. And, of course, receiving Reiki treatments during her visits, and working with crystals, essential oils, and mindset shifts didn't hurt, either! Ms. M's experience teaches us that our healing journey often takes time. As we peel back our layers of our complexity, like an onion, we reveal many layers underneath.

While healing multiple chakras simultaneously can take some time, it can be done. Here are some ways to use crystals, breathwork, visualizations, essential oils, and yoga to work on multiple chakras.

Meditation

First, lie down. As you relax, practice directing a slow inhale into your root chakra, slowly exhaling its energy through your mouth. Do this breathing exercise three times, allowing each exhale to release anything you may be storing in that chakra. If you like, you can place your hands on the lower aspect of your hips during this exercise. Allow yourself to get in touch with any emotions that may be stored in that chakra. Or, perhaps you may notice some physical discomfort. Just observe what you are sensing there. Then visualize a red sphere of light at that chakra—whirling, spinning, and pulsing. Imagine it growing and becoming more vibrant, radiating healing light into your root chakra. Notice if the sensation you initially felt there has changed after the breathwork and visualizations. Repeat for all the chakras, with their corresponding location and color, ending at the crown chakra.

Crystals

If you have crystals with you, you can also turn the previous exercise into a "crystal bath" by first placing the crystals for single chakras on each respective chakra, then working through the breathing exercises.

Besides a crystal bath, you may also be able to heal multiple chakras with a single crystal. Selenite is a wonderful crystal—one that clears debris in the energy body and helps overcome stagnation, allowing you to communicate more clearly with your Higher Self. (For crystal images, see the Appendix on page 158.)

While selenite comes in many forms, use its wand form to address multiple chakras. Place it on the midline of your body, straight down the center, wherever feels right. Or, for a good basic placement, lay the crystal down your midline, so it touches your heart chakra, solar plexus chakra, and, if it's long enough, the sacral plexus chakra. By using the selenite wand in this way, you create an energetic alignment of the chakras, even with those energy centers the selenite is not physically touching.

Essential Oils

When using essential oils to address multiple chakras, anoint each chakra with one or more oil used to reach each one. Start at the root chakra and work your way up to the crown chakra. If you want to treat very specific chakras at the same time, just anoint those. You might also try creating a blend of essential oils that can treat multiple chakras at once. Whatever you decide, always remember to use a carrier oil when working with essential oils to avoid skin irritation.

Yoga

Because yoga works to unite the breath with body awareness and movement, a single yoga class, depending on its style, can address multiple chakras at once. Infusing breath while moving the body into specific poses can open multiple energy centers at the same time. (For illustrations of yoga poses, see the Appendix on page 146.)

YOGA POSES

• • • • • • •

The following yoga poses can be helpful for balancing your chakras. For yoga poses that engage one side of the body, practice the same pose on the other side of the body, too, to maintain symmetry and balance.

BOAT POSE

Begin seated, with your knees bent and together, and your shins parallel to the ground. Maintain a long spine with a lifted chest. Stretch your hands forward energetically, reaching for the knees. To advance, straighten the legs and lift your feet skyward.

BOUND ANGLE POSE

Begin seated, with the soles of your feet pressed together. Lengthen your spine. Fold forward, and reach your forehead towards your toes.

BRIDGE POSE

Lying on your back, with your knees bent and feet hip-width apart, engage your pelvic floor muscles and abdomen. Energetically draw the heels towards your head and press your feet downward. Raise your hips up. Option: Interlace your hands underneath your body to open the chest/shoulders.

CAMEL POSE

Begin kneeling, with your knees hip-width apart. Place your hands on your lower back, with your fingers pointing upward. Draw your palms downward energetically to lengthen the spine. Lift your heart towards sky. To advance: Make your hands hold the heels.

CAT POSE

Begin in tabletop position. Round your spine skyward, and tuck the chin and tailbone under. Draw your navel in and up towards the spine.

CHAIR POSE

Begin standing with your feet together. Weight is on the heels. Move the hips downward. Sweep your arms skyward, maintaining a neutral spine.

CHILD'S POSE

Begin in tabletop position. Sink your hips to your heels. Stretch your arms back towards your feet, alongside the body, with the palms facing up. Rest your head on the ground and relax.

COW FACE POSE

Sit tall, with your right knee stacked atop the other and hips laterally rotated. Your sitz bones should remain grounded. Reach your right arm behind the head, and reach your left arm behind the back. Try to clasp your hands together. Option for stiff shoulders: Use a towel or yoga strap to reach your hands closer together.

COW POSE

Begin in tabletop position. Arch your back, and drop the belly downward. Maintain length throughout your spine. Gaze upward, and intend the crown of your head skyward.

DOWNWARD FACING DOG

Begin in plank position. Raise your hips skyward, with all ten fingers pressed firmly into the ground. Depress your shoulders, bring the chest towards your thighs, and tuck your navel in. Lengthen your legs, and reach down with your heels. Feel the many opposing directional pulls.

EAGLE POSE

Begin in Chair Pose. Double bind the arms and legs. Lengthen your spine, and sink deeply into the knees. Square your shoulders and hips forward. Option for stiff shoulders: Bear hug yourself. Option for stiff hips: Single wrap the legs, and energetically intend towards a double bind.

EXTENDED SIDE ANGLE

From Warrior II on the right side, release your forward hand to the ground, and rest your forearm on your mid-thigh. Extend your opposite arm over your ear, with your palm facing down. Gaze up towards your left hand, if possible.

FOUR LIMBED STAFF POSTURE

*Requires shoulder stability and strong abdominal strength

From Plank Pose, shift your weight so that your shoulders are slightly ahead of the wrists. Bend your elbows 90 degrees, and press your upper arms into your body (being sure your arms are aligned with your body). Make sure your forearms are perpendicular to the ground, and your chest remains broad. Strongly engage your abdominals to maintain your body in plank.

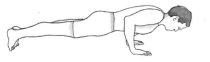

HALF BOAT POSE

From Boat Pose, bring your hands to a prayer position. Bring your upper body and legs lower a few inches from the ground. Strongly engage your abdominal section.

HAPPY BABY POSE

Lying on your back, bend your knees and reach for the outer edges of your feet. Draw the knees and tailbone downward. Bring the soles of your feet skyward, with the shins perpendicular to the ground. Option: Rock side to side like a baby.

HEAD-TO-KNEE POSE

Sit on the floor, with your legs extended in front of you, and your back and legs at a 90-degree angle. Draw your right foot toward the groin. Release your knee to the floor, with your foot flush against your inner thigh. Fold forward to hold your ankle or foot.

HEADSTAND

*Do not attempt if you have any neck or shoulder conditions

Interlace the hands, with your palm heels pressed together. Nestle the crown of your head on the ground between the "V" of your fore-arms. Walk your feet towards your head. Engage the abdominals and pelvic floor muscles to float your legs skyward. Balance your weight mostly on the forearms, and less on the head and neck.

OPEN ANGLE POSE

Begin seated. Straddle your legs very widely, with your toes pointing skyward. Maintain a lifted and lengthened spine. Fold forward between your legs. Rest on your forearms or the ground, with your arms outstretched.

PIGEON POSE

From plank position, move your right shin directly behind your hands (parallel to the top of the mat). To protect the knee, dorsiflex your ankle (draw the toes toward the knee). Release your back leg to the ground, and energetically reach your toes backward. To deepen, drop to your forearms or release your body to the ground, with your arms stretched forward.

PLOW POSE

* Do not attempt if you have a neck condition

Begin seated. Draw the navel in, and roll onto your back. Send the legs straight behind your head, with your toes landing on the floor. Support your lower back with your hands, or press the arms down on the ground.

RECLINING BOUND ANGLE POSE

Lying on your back, press the soles of your feet together with your knees pointed outward. If your knees do not touch the ground easily, place pillows or blocks to support them. Your arms may rest on your belly, by your sides, or stretch backwards.

SEATED SPINAL TWIST

Seated on the floor, extend your legs in front of you, with your back and legs at a 90-degree angle. Cross your right foot to the outside of your left knee, and seal your foot to the ground. Option: Bend the left knee so your foot is outside the right hip. Wrap your left arm around the bent knee. Option: Press the left elbow against the outside of your knee. Twist, and gaze behind your right shoulder. Inhale to lift and lengthen the spine, and exhale to twist more deeply.

SHOULDERSTAND

* Do not attempt if you have a neck condition

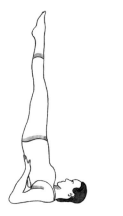

Seated on the floor, draw your navel in, and roll onto your back. Send the legs and torso straight skyward. Support the lower back with your hands or press your hands down on the ground.

STANDING FORWARD BEND

Begin standing, with your feet together or hip-width apart. Fold forward from your hip joint, maintaining a lengthened spine. Place your hands flat on the ground, or hold them behind the ankles to deepen your posture.

SUPPORTED CHILD'S POSE

You may use bolsters or pillows beneath your body to deepen the comfort of Child's Pose. Rest and relax.

SUPPORTED CORPSE POSE

You may use any combination of bolsters, pillows, sandbags, or blankets to deepen the comfort of Corpse Pose— under the knees, lower back, wrists, and head, or on your belly, eyes, or palms. Use a blanket to keep warm. Get cozy so you can rest deeply.

SUPPORTED FORWARD BEND

Begin seated, with your arms straight at your sides and your palms flat on the floor. Stretch your legs in front of you, and point your toes at the ceiling. Fold forward over a large pillow or bolster, and allow your entire upper body to relax.

TREE POSE

Begin standing, and transfer your weight to the right foot. Float the left leg up, and place your foot high on the right inner thigh, with your toes pointing downward. Place your hands in prayer position at your heart center.

TRIANGLE POSE

Begin standing, and spread your arms wide with the feet parallel 3-4 feet apart. Turn your right foot out 90 degrees, and gaze over the middle finger of the right hand. Reach far right, drop the hand to your shin or your palm to the ground. Stretch your left hand skyward. Stack your hips one atop the other.

WARRIOR I

Begin standing, with your feet hip-width apart. Step the left foot back 4-5 feet, and seal your foot to the ground (with your toes turned out 30-45 degrees). Sink into your right knee 90 degrees. Square the shoulders and hips forward. Sweep your arms up, with the palms facing each other. Maintain a neutral low spine. Gaze upward towards your hands—the heart lifts skyward.

WARRIOR 2

Begin standing, and spread your arms wide, with the feet parallel 4-5 feet apart. Turn your right foot 90 degrees, and sink the front-facing knee to a 90-degree angle. Seal the outer edge of your left foot flat on the ground, with your leg remaining straight. Gaze over the middle finger of your right hand, keeping your spine erect.

SUN SALUTATION

Standing tall, inhale and raise your arms up. Exhale, and fold forward over, keeping the legs straight. Inhale, and gaze forward with your hands on your shins. Exhale, and move into plank position—lower your knees, chest, and chin to the ground. Inhale, and move into Cobra or Upward Facing Dog. Exhale, and move into Downward Facing Dog. Remain here for up to five breaths. Inhale, and step or jump your feet between your hands. Exhale into Standing Forward Fold. Inhale, stand tall, and raise your arms up. Exhale, and bring your hands to your sides or to prayer position.

CRYSTALS

● ● · ● · ● · ●

Crystal healing can be a powerful way of working with chakras.
Use the following images and descriptions to help you decide
which crystals best suit your needs.

AMBER

Amber is a great stone to fortify the
sacral plexus and solar plexus chakras.
The more yellow the hue, the better it
would be for the solar plexus chakras.
The more orange the hue, the better it
would be for the sacral plexus chakra.

AMETHYST

Amethyst is usually the first stone people
are attracted to when learning about
crystals. It corresponds with the third eye
and crown chakras, and is very calming.
It helps to cultivate our intuition and
prevents against psychic attacks.

APOPHYLLITE

This stone is most commonly colorless,
white, or gray, but sometimes apophyllite appears in a rare green hue. This
high-vibrational stone corresponds to the
crown chakra, and helps us enhance our
psychic abilities. It is especially good at
clearing blockages in the crown chakra.

AQUAMARINE

Aquamarine corresponds to the throat chakra, and is a blue or blue-green color. It assists us in clear communications by activating the throat chakra, and is very calming and cooling on physical and emotional levels.

BLACK TOURMALINE

Black tourmaline is a great stone for the root chakra, because it is very grounding. However, it is best known as the premiere stone for psychic protection, since it deflects all negative energies that are directed to you. This should be worn on the body.

BLOODSTONE

This stone strengthens the root chakra, and helps you to fully ground yourself in your body. It is dark green with red spots and blotches. It is a stone of vitality, and helps endurance and strength. It also helps with all types of blood disorders.

BLUE KYANITE

Blue kyanite is a highly vibrating stone that helps heal the throat chakra. Because it also opens psychic channels, this stone happens to help the third eye chakra as well. It can easily be spotted with its distinctive elongated, flat, bladelike striations.

CARNELIAN

Carnelian is an orange-colored stone that activates the sacral plexus chakra. When carnelian has a dark red hue to it, it can also address the root chakra. If it has yellower tones, it also resonates with the solar plexus chakra.

CELESTITE

Celestite's most frequent color is gray-blue. It activates the throat chakra, though it also heals the other higher chakras in the body, such as the third eye and crown. It is a good stone to use when contacting spirit guides and angels.

CLEAR QUARTZ

Clear quartz is a great multi-purpose stone that addresses all chakras, but it is especially useful for healing the crown chakra. This stone is a great amplifier, and can be placed by other stones to augment their healing properties.

CORAL (RED)

Coral comes in many colors, but the red coral featured here opens and activates the root chakra. It can also strengthen the circulatory system and bones in the body, and stimulate our metabolic processes to help release impurities from the muscular system.

EMERALD

Emerald is a strong heart healer on emotional and physical levels, and stimulates love, compassion, healing, and abundance. It is the stone that most purely represents the energy patterns of the activated heart chakra.

FLUORITE

Fluorite can be found in many colors, and often has multiple colors in the same specimen. All shades enhance mental clarity and clear energy fields. It heals all chakras, depending on the colors it possesses, but is most often associated with the third eye chakra.

FIRE AGATE

Fire agate is mostly associated with the root chakra, which it activates, but it also stimulates the sacral plexus and solar plexus chakras. It is a multi-colored stone that has a deep brown base hue with flashes of orange, red, green, and gold.

GARNET

Garnet comes in a wide range of colors, but is most commonly associated with its red version, which is very stabilizing to the root chakra. It provides purification and cleansing of areas in our lives that are chaotic, and can treat disorders of the spine, bone, and blood.

GREEN CALCITE

Calcite comes in many colors, and the green version stimulates the heart chakra. It clears the heart chakra of stress, and helps promote relaxation, emotional balance, and connection with the heart.

GREEN KYANITE

Green kyanite connects us to our heart chakra, helping us to find the truth of our hearts and guiding us to live from that truth. This stone forms flat, bladelike crystals. Note: Green kyanite should not be cleaned with salt water, or it will get damaged.

GREEN TOURMALINE

Green tourmaline can vary in color from pastel green to dark olive. It heals the heart chakra, and is one of the premiere stones for self-healing. It promotes balance with the body, and is a great stone to enhance the health of houseplants.

HEMATITE

Hematite strongly secures our root chakra, and is perhaps the most effective stone that helps us ground ourselves in our bodies and the physical world. It harmonizes easily with other grounding stones such as black tourmaline and smoky quartz.

HERKIMER DIAMOND

Herkimer diamonds are usually clear, but can have inclusions or be more smoky than colorless. They activate and open the crown chakra, and are manifestations of pure spiritual light. This stone helps us purify our energy fields and stay focused while meditating.

IOLITE

Iolite often appears violet, or clear bluish-lavender. It opens up the light pathway from the throat chakra to the crown chakra, and is therefore associated with the throat, third eye, and crown chakras. It is effective for shamanic journeying and healing old wounds.

JADE

Jade comes in various colors, but the green variety is most popular. Green jade harmonizes and balances the heart chakra, and is a stone for healing the heart. It fosters steady growth of life force energy, otherwise known as qi.

KUNZITE

Kunzite resonates with the crown and heart chakras, and aligns the energy of the mind with that of the heart. It aids in grounding our beliefs, enhances intuition, and helps us lift confusion. It opens the heart to the energies of love.

KYANITE

There are various colors of kyanite, which are generally healing to all chakras. Blue kyanite works with the throat chakra and third eye chakra, while green kyanite connects to the heart chakra.

LABRADORITE

Labradorite is full of vivid flashes of green blue, gold, orange, red, and even violet at times. It is the gemstone of magic (meaning our intuitive gifts). Wearing it enhances our innate abilities. It assists all chakras, but is especially helpful for the crown chakra.

LAPIS LAZULI

This stone activates the third eye and throat chakras. It is a stone for clairvoyance and precognition. It is a deep blue, with gold and sometimes white flecks. Place it over your third eye to help you gain insight into your dreams.

LEPIDOLITE

The color of lepidolite is often pink or purplish. It resonates with all chakras, but activates the third eye and heart chakras. It is a stone of serenity and spiritual purification. Meditating with it can clear blocked energies in any of the chakras.

LODESTONE

Lodestone, a form of magnetite, powerfully grounds the root chakra. It is also said to strengthen the circulatory system, and helps blood disorders. It is easily identified because it is often covered with small particles of magnetite and other magnetic minerals.

MOONSTONE

Moonstone has a blue-white sheen. It can reveal to women their feminine power and their connection to the goddess. When used by males, it stimulates the right side of the brain, which encourages emotional balance. It activates the crown chakra.

OBSIDIAN

Black obsidian is the most common of the obsidian variations, and comes in a black, glossy color. It is grounding for the root chakra, and powerfully eliminates negative energies within ourselves and our environment. It's also very protective, and cleanses the auric field of disharmony.

ONYX

There are a few types of onyx, but it's the black onyx that we are most familiar with. Black onyx stimulates the first chakra, and grounds us into the electromagnetic energy of the Earth. It calms and condenses excessive energies, which eases anxiety.

ORANGE TOURMALINE

Tourmaline comes in many variations and colors. Orange tourmaline stimulates the sacral plexus chakra and enhances creativity, intuition of the physical plane, and sexuality. It is very rare, and usually occurs with yellow and red colors.

PERIDOT

Peridot ranges from olive to lime green in color. It harmonizes the heart chakra, as well as the solar plexus chakras. It helps us receive Universal Love, which helps us receive abundance on all levels of life.

PHENACITE

Phenacite is a rare mineral that can easily be mistaken for other stones, such as quartz or topaz. This stone is a powerful generator of pure White Light energy, and activates the crown and third eye chakras.

RED JASPER

Red jasper opens and stimulates the root chakra and powerfully grounds us to the Earth. This stone's frequency can stimulate one's kundalini energy. Note: Raising kundalini energy should be done gradually!

ROSE QUARTZ

Rose quartz is the premiere love stone. It activates the heart chakra, and helps us tap into love for others in our lives, the community, the Earth, the Universe, the Divine, and our knowledge of self-love. It gently, but powerfully, helps us heal our hearts.

RUBY

Ruby powerfully stimulates the root chakra, and helps bring life force and vitality into our being. Wear ruby if you want to activate your physical, mental, and emotional bodies. It instills courage, and stimulates the flow of life force energy, or qi, through the body.

RUTILATED QUARTZ

Rutilated quartz resonates with all chakras, but is most often associated with the solar plexus chakra. It helps to stabilize emotional and mental processes, and can be used to stabilize the digestive system and improve nutrient absorption.

SELENITE

Selenite is effective at cleansing the auric field, and is great for any energy clearing work. It quickly activates the crown chakra, as well as the third eye chakra. It is often seen in wand form.

SMOKY QUARTZ

Smoky quartz is a powerfully grounding and clearing stone. It activates and opens the root chakra, and clears the aura and energetic systems. It absorbs and transmutes negativity by grounding it in the Earth.

SODALITE

This deep blue stone activates the throat chakra, as well as the third eye chakra. It helps us open to our truth, and improves communication. It reduces negativity, and enhances positivity. Hoarseness and throat discomfort may be improved by using sodalite.

STAR SAPPHIRE

Star sapphire activates the third eye. It enhances the centering of our thoughts, and is known as a stone of wisdom and good luck. Meditate with this over your third eye to feel its effects.

SUGILITE

Sugilite powerfully opens the third eye chakra, as well as the crown chakra. It has numerous beneficial qualities, is protective and purifying, and activates the heart and mind. It helps us overcome hopelessness, and the feeling that we don't have options in life.

SUNSTONE

The sunstone gets its name from its warm color and reflected light, which reminds us of the sun. It energizes the sacral plexus chakra, as well as the solar plexus chakra. Sunstone stimulates creativity and sexuality.

TANZANITE

Tanzanite activates the third eye and crown chakras. It integrates the energies of the mind and heart, which helps us stay centered in our wisdom. The most common varieties range in hue from blue to blue-violet, though some are golden to brownish yellow as well.

TURQUOISE

Turquoise is probably the longest-used of all gemstones. It resonates with our throat chakra, and wearing one can empower those of us who are shy about sharing ourselves with the world. It is a stone for forgiveness.

WHITE TOPAZ

Otherwise known as colorless topaz, white topaz stimulates the crown chakra, and assists us in honing our psychic and intuitive gifts. It can help those who have difficulty telling the truth due to fear, or others who need help learning their personal truth.

YELLOW AGATE

Yellow agate harmonizes the solar plexus chakra, and helps us cultivate courage, self-confidence, and strength. It may also aid with digestive issues, such as food allergies and metabolism, and increase concentration and memory.

YELLOW CITRINE

Citrine can range in hue from pale yellow to almost orange—and some may have brownish tinges. Yellow citrine stimulates the solar plexus chakra, and strengthens our will. It powerfully purifies our center.

YELLOW TIGER'S EYE

Yellow tiger's eye stimulates the third eye chakra. It is a stone of vitality, practicality, mental clarity, and physical action. It helps us respond to our needs and challenges in life while remaining grounded.

YELLOW TOPAZ

Yellow topaz activates the solar plexus chakra, and strongly strengthens our will. It helps us manifest that which we want to create in life, and helps to calm stress and irritability. When using this stone, it's best to wear it on the body.

RESOURCES

• • • • • • •

Brennan, Barbara Ann. *Hands of Light: A Guide to Healing Through the Human Energy Field*. New York, NY: Bantam Books, 1988. A thorough resource on the dynamics of energy in the human energy field, including the human aura, and tools to develop the healer.

Bruyere, Rosalyn L. *Wheels of Light: Chakras, Auras, and the Healing Energy of the Body*. Simon and Schuster, 1994. An insightful understanding of the energy body, vibration, and chakras for healers and those looking to heal.

Hay, Louise L. *You Can Heal Your Life*. Hay House, Inc., 1999. A classic, thoughtful manual on healing yourself through self-love and transforming your thought processes.

Judith, Anodea, PhD. *Wheels of Life: The Classic Guide to the Chakra System*. Llewellyn Publications, 1999. A classic, in-depth exploration of the chakra system.

Melody. *Love Is in the Earth: A Kaleidoscope of Crystals*. Wheat Ridge, CO: Earth-Love Publishing House, 1995. A comprehensive resource on the metaphysical properties of crystals.

Mercier, Patricia. *Chakras: Balance Your Body's Energy for Health and Harmony*. Godsfield Press, 2000. Provides basic groundwork to understanding the chakra system.

Myss, Caroline. *Anatomy of the Spirit: The Seven Stages of Power and Healing*. New York, NY: Harmony Books, 1996. Dr. Myss draws upon three spiritual traditions—the Hindu chakras, the Christian sacraments, and the Kabbalah's Tree of Life—to describe a model of the body's seven centers of spiritual and physical power.

Simmons, Robert, and Naisha Ahsian. *The Book of Stones: Who They Are and What They Teach*. North Atlantic Books, 2007. A comprehensive crystal text.

Wauters, Ambika. *Chakras and Their Archetypes: Uniting Energy Awareness and Spiritual Growth*. The Crossing Press, 1997. Covers the positive and negative archetypes of each chakra.

REFERENCES

• • • • • • •

Brennan, Barbara Ann. *Hands of Light: A Guide to Healing Through the Human Energy Field*. New York, NY: Bantam Books, 1988.

Fennell, Alexander B., Erik M. Benau, and Ruth Ann Atchley. "A Single Session of Meditation Reduces Physiological Indices of Anger in Both Experienced and Novice Meditators." *Consciousness and Cognition* 40 (February 2016):54–66. doi: 10.1016/j.concog.2015.12.010.

Hay, Louise L. *You Can Heal Your Life*. Carlsbad, CA: Hay House, Inc., 1999.

Judith, Anodea, PhD. *Wheels of Life: The Classic Guide to the Chakra System*. Woodbury, MN: Llewellyn Publications, 1999.

Mayo Clinic. "Diseases and Conditions: Cancer. Risk Factors." Accessed September 21, 2016. www.mayoclinic.org/diseases-conditions /cancer/basics/risk-factors/con-20032378.

Mayo Clinic. "Diseases and Conditions: Hemorrhoids." Accessed September 21, 2016. www.mayoclinic.org/diseases-conditions/hemorrhoids /home/ovc-20249172.

Mayo Clinic. "Diseases and Conditions: Uterine Fibroids." Accessed September 21, 2016. www.mayoclinic.org/diseases-conditions /uterine-fibroids/home/ovc-20212509.

Melody. *Love Is in the Earth: A Kaleidoscope of Crystals*. Wheat Ridge, CO: Earth-Love Publishing House, 1995.

Mercier, Patricia. *Chakras: Balance Your Body's Energy for Health and Harmony*. New York, NY: Godsfield Press, 2000.

Simmons, Robert, and Naisha Ahsian. *The Book of Stones: Who They Are and What They Teach*. Berkeley, CA: North Atlantic Books, 2007.

Wauters, Ambika. *Chakras and Their Archetypes: Uniting Energy Awareness and Spiritual Growth*. Berkeley, CA: The Crossing Press, 1977.

INDEX

• • • • • • •

A

abdomen, 27
abundance, 24, 94
acceptance and tolerance, 26
acupuncture, 47
addiction, 31, 55
adrenal fatigue, 56
adrenal glands, 23, 27
affirmations
  "I am," 23
  "I can," 27
  "I feel," 25
  "I know," 35
  "I love," 29
  "I see," 33
  "I speak," 31
  See symptoms and ailments,
    common
air, chakra associated with, 29
ajna, 33
alienation, 35
altar space, blessing, 50–51
amber, 25, 27, 97, 105
amethyst, 33, 35, 129, 137
anahata, 29
ancestors, keeping photos of, 50–51
anger, 56–57. *See also* conflict
  sacral plexus chakra, 24
  solar plexus chakra, 27
  toward the Divine, 35
anorexia, 27, 57–58
anxiety, 58–59. *See also* panic attacks
apathy, 35
apophyllite, 35, 137
appearances, keeping up, 26

appendix, 25
aquamarine, 31, 121
arms, 29, 31
arthritis, 23, 27
asanas, practicing, 41. *See also* yoga
asthma and allergies, 29, 59
auras, clearing, 50
awareness, 32

B

back pain, 59–60. *See also* sciatica
base chakra. *See* root chakra
behavioral changes, making, 39–40
being, chakra associated with, 19
bergamot essential oil, 29, 115
black tourmaline, 23, 89
bladder, 25
blame, 25
blindness, 33
bloodstone, 23, 89
blue, chakra associated with, 31
blue kyanite, 31, 121
blurred vision, 33
body parts. *See* physical body parts
bowl of offering, using, 51
brain, 33
brain tumors, 61
breast cancer, 29, 61
bronchial pneumonia, 29
brow chakra. *See* third eye chakra
bulimia, 27, 57–58

C

calm and peace, 26
cancer, 61
candles, lighting, 51

care of self and others, 27
carnelian, 25, 97
celestite, 31, 121
central nervous system, 35
cerebral cortex, 35
cervical cancer, 61
chakra healing
    myths, 17
    power of, 16
    warnings, 17–18
chakra system, foundation of, 19
chakras
    awakening, 20–21
    as energy vortexes, 14
    feeling, 15
    Sanskrit derivation, 13–14
    spiritual versus physical, 19
chanting mantra sounds
    crown chakra, 141
    heart chakra, 117
    root chakra, 93
    sacral plexus chakra, 101
    solar plexus chakra, 109
    third eye chakra, 133
    throat chakra, 125
circulatory system, 29
cleaning crystals, 89
clear quartz, 33, 35, 129, 137
codependency, 62
colon/intestinal problems, 27
colors of chakras
    crown chakra, 35
    heart chakra, 29
    root chakra, 23
    sacral plexus chakra, 25
    solar plexus chakra, 27
    third eye chakra, 33
    throat chakra, 31
communication, chakra associated
    with, 19

compassion, chakra associated with,
    19, 29, 110
conflict, 63. *See also* anger
confusion, 35
congestive heart failure, 29
connection, experiencing, 29, 86
constipation, 23, 63–64
control and dominance, 26–27
coral, 25, 97
courage, 35
creativity, 19, 25, 31, 94
criticism, sensitivity to, 27, 31
crown chakra
    affirmation, 35
    cancers, 61
    causes of energy blocks, 35
    chanting mantra, 141
    characteristics, 134
    color, 35
    crystals, 35, 137–138
    depression, 64
    element, 35
    essential oils, 35, 139
    fatigue, 66
    glands, 35
    headaches, 68–69
    life lessons, 35
    location, 35
    meditation, 135–136
    mental/emotional issues, 35
    names, 35
    in and out of harmony, 34
    physical body parts and
        dysfunctions, 35
    purpose of, 19
    Sanskrit name, 35
    skin issues, 79–80
    stress, 81
    tips, 141
    yoga, 140

crystals
  allies, 50
  amber, 25, 27, 97, 105
  amethyst, 33, 35, 129, 137
  apophyllite, 35, 137
  aquamarine, 31, 121
  black tourmaline, 23, 89
  bloodstone, 23, 89
  blue kyanite, 31, 121
  carnelian, 25, 97
  celestite, 31, 121
  cleaning, 89
  clear quartz, 33, 35, 129, 137
  coral, 25, 97
  crown chakra, 35, 137–138
  emerald, 29, 113
  fire agate, 23, 89
  fluorite, 33, 129
  garnet, 23, 89
  green calcite, 29, 113
  green kyanite, 29, 113
  green tourmaline, 29, 113
  heart chakra, 113–114
  hematite, 23, 89
  Herkimer diamond, 35, 137
  iolite, 31, 121
  jade, 29, 113
  kunzite, 35, 137
  kyanite, 33, 129
  labradorite, 35, 137
  lapis lazuli, 31, 33, 121, 129
  lepidolite, 33, 129
  lodestone, 23, 89
  moonstone, 25, 35, 97, 137
  obsidian, 23, 89
  onyx, 23, 89
  orange tourmaline, 25, 97
  peridot, 29, 113
  phenacite, 35, 137
  red jasper, 23, 89
  root chakra, 89–90
  rose quartz, 29, 113
  ruby, 23, 89
  rutilated quartz, 27, 105
  sacral plexus chakra, 97–98
  selenite, 35, 137
  smoky quartz, 23, 89
  sodalite, 31, 121
  solar plexus chakra, 105–106
  star sapphire, 33, 129
  sugilite, 33, 129
  sunstone, 25, 97
  tanzanite, 33, 129
  third eye chakra, 33
  throat chakra, 31, 121–122
  turquoise, 31, 121
  using, 43–44, 144–145
  white topaz, 35, 137
  yellow agate, 27, 105
  yellow citrine, 27, 105
  yellow tiger's eye, 27, 105
  yellow topaz, 27, 105

D
deafness, 33
decision-making responsibility, 27, 31
depression, 23, 28, 35, 64
devotion, 35
diabetes/pancreatitis, 27
diaphragm, 29
diet and food, 46, 48
digestive issues, chakras affected, 65
disconnection from self and others,
  65–66
Divine, 34–35, 134
dominance and control, 26
dreams, following, 30–31

E
ears, 33
earth, association with root chakra, 23
eating disorders, 57–58
emerald, 29, 113

emotional intelligence, 33
emotions, connecting to, 25, 94. *See also* mental/emotional issues
energetic disorders, 35
energy
    clearing, 50
    maintaining through movement, 49
energy blocks
    crown chakra, 35
    heart chakra, 29
    root chakra, 23
    sacral plexus chakra, 25
    solar plexus chakra, 27
    third eye chakra, 33
    throat chakra, 31
energy body, 13–14
enlightenment, seeking, 20–21
Epsom salt baths, taking, 49–50
esophagus, 31
essential oils
    bergamot, 29, 115
    crown chakra, 35, 139
    frankincense, 31, 33, 35, 123, 131, 139
    geranium, 29, 115
    German chamomile, 31, 123
    heart chakra, 29
    heart chakra, 29, 115
    hyssop, 31, 123
    lavender, 27, 29, 31, 33, 107, 115, 123, 131
    lemon, 25, 27, 99, 107
    lotus, 35, 139
    melissa/lemon balm, 29, 115
    myrrh, 23, 91
    neroli, 29, 115
    palmarosa, 29, 115
    patchouli, 23, 25, 91, 99
    peppermint, 35, 139
    Roman chamomile, 27, 107
    root chakra, 23, 91

rose, 29, 115
rosemary, 27, 31, 107, 123
rosewood, 25, 27, 99, 107
sacral plexus chakra, 25
sacral plexus chakra, 99
sandalwood, 23, 25, 33, 35, 91, 99, 131, 139
solar plexus chakra, 27
solar plexus chakra, 107
spikenard, 23, 91
third eye chakra, 33
throat chakra, 31, 123
using, 44–46, 145
vetiver, 23, 91
ylang ylang, 25, 29, 99, 115
ethics, 25
exhaustion, 35
eyes, 33

F
faith, 31, 35
family, 19
fatigue, 27, 66
fear, 27, 57, 66–67
feather wand, using, 50
feeling chakras, 15
feelings, difficulty expressing, 24
fifth chakra. *See* throat chakra
fire, chakra associated with, 27
fire agate, 23, 89
first chakra. *See* root chakra
fluorite, 33, 129
food and diet, 46, 48
forehead chakra. *See* third eye chakra
forgiveness, 29
fourth chakra. *See* heart chakra
frankincense essential oil, 31, 33, 35, 123, 131, 139

G
gallbladder, 27
garnet, 23, 89

genitals, 25
geranium essential oil, 29, 115
German chamomile essential oil, 31, 123
glands
    crown chakra, 35
    heart chakra, 29
    root chakra, 23
    sacral plexus chakra, 25
    solar plexus chakra, 27
    third eye chakra, 33
    throat chakra, 31
God/dess, disconnection from, 34
gold, chakra associated with, 35
gratefulness, practicing, 49
green, chakra associated with, 29
green calcite, 29, 113
green kyanite, 29, 113
green tourmaline, 29, 113
grief, 29, 67–68
grounding, 86
guilt, 25, 68
gums and teeth, 31

H

habits, changing, 39–40
hands
    and throat chakra, 31
    warmth and energy exchange, 15
hatred and love, 29. *See also* self-hate
headaches, 33, 68–69
healing practitioner, getting help
    from, 18
healing space, creating, 50–51
heart attack, 29
heart chakra
    affirmation, 29
    asthma/allergies, 59
    back pain, 60
    cancers, 61
    causes of energy blocks, 29

chanting mantra, 117
characteristics, 110
codependency, 62
color, 29
crystals, 29, 113–114
depression, 64
disconnection issues, 65–66
element, 29
essential oils, 29, 115
gland, 29
grief, 67–68
life lessons, 29
location, 29
loneliness, 72–73
meditations, 111–112
mental/emotional issues, 29
names, 29
in and out of harmony, 28
panic attacks, 74–75
physical body parts and
    dysfunctions, 29
purpose of, 19
Sanskrit names, 29
self-hate, 76
stress, 81
tips, 117
yoga, 116
heart disease, 29
heartache, 29
hematite, 23, 89
hemorrhoids, 23, 69–70
hepatitis, 27
Herkimer diamond, 35, 137
high blood pressure, 29
hip pain, 25, 70
honor, 27
hope, 29
HUM, chanting, 125
hypothalamus, 31
hyssop essential oil, 31, 123

I

"I am" affirmation, 23
"I can" affirmation, 27
"I feel" affirmation, 25
"I know" affirmation, 35
"I love" affirmation, 29
"I see" affirmation, 33
"I speak" affirmation, 31
immune-related disorders, 23
inadequacy, feelings of, 26
indigestion, 27
indigo, chakra associated with, 33
infertility, 70–71
Inner Divine, 134
inner vision, 126
inner voice, listening to, 30
inner warrior fire, 102
insight and intuition, 33
inspiration, 35
intellectual abilities, 33
intestines, 27
intimidation, 27
intuition, chakra associated with, 19, 32, 126
iolite, 31, 121

J

jade, 29, 113
jaw pain, 71–72
joy, cultivating, 110
judgment, 31

K

kidneys, 25
knee problems, 23
Kundalini energy, 20–21, 41
kunzite, 35, 137
kyanite, 33, 129

L

labradorite, 35, 137
LAM, chanting, 93

lapis lazuli, 31, 33, 121, 129
lavender essential oil, 27, 29, 31, 33, 107, 115, 123, 131
learning disabilities, 33
leg pain, 72
lemon essential oil, 25, 27, 99, 107
lepidolite, 33, 129
life lessons
    crown chakra, 35
    heart chakra, 29
    root chakra, 23
    sacral plexus chakra, 25
    solar plexus chakra, 27
    third eye chakra, 33
    throat chakra, 31
life task, living, 27
lifestyle changes, making, 39–40
light
    chakra associated with, 33
    sensitivity to, 35
liver, 27
lodestone, 23, 89
loneliness, 29, 72–73
lotus essential oil, 35, 139
love
    chakra associated with, 19
    and hatred, 29
lower back
    chakras affected, 60
    pain, 23
lower vertebrae, 25
lung cancer, 29, 61
lung disease, 29
lungs, 29

M

magnesium, benefits of, 50
manipura, 27
mantras. *See* chanting mantra sounds
meditation
    crown chakra, 135–136

heart chakra, 111–112
implementing, 38
practicing, 38, 144
pros/cons, 38
purpose, 37–38
root chakra, 87–88
sacral plexus chakra, 95–96
solar plexus chakra, 103–104
third eye chakra, 127–128
throat chakra, 119–120
melissa/lemon balm essential oil,
    29, 115
mental/emotional issues. *See also*
    emotions
    crown chakra, 35
    heart chakra, 29
    root chakra, 23
    sacral plexus chakra, 25
    solar plexus chakra, 27
    third eye chakra, 33
    throat chakra, 31
middle back, chakras affected, 60
middle spine, 27
mindfulness, cultivating, 49
money, issues around, 24–25
moonstone, 25, 35, 97, 137
mouth, 31
movement, using to maintain energy,
    49
muladhara, 23
muscular system, 35
myrrh, 23, 91

N

nature, trust and mistrust of, 22
naval chakra. *See* sacral plexus chakra
neck pain, 73–74
neck vertebrae, 31
needs, communicating, 118
negative energy, clearing, 49
neroli essential oil, 29, 115

nervous system, 33
neurological disturbances, 33
neuropathy, 74
nose, 33

O

obsidian, 23, 89
OM, chanting, 141
onyx, 23, 89
orange, chakra associated with, 25
orange tourmaline, 25, 97
ovaries, 25

P

palmarosa essential oil, 29, 115
Palo Santo, using, 50
pancreatitis/diabetes, 27
panic attacks, 74–75. *See also* anxiety
parathyroid gland, 31
patchouli essential oil, 23, 25, 91, 99
patience, cultivating, 17–18
peace and calm, 26
pelvis, 25. *See also* sacral plexus chakra
peppermint essential oil, 35, 139
pericardium, 29
peridot, 29, 113
personal power, 26, 31
personality, 26
phenacite, 35, 137
photos, keeping, 50–51
physical body parts and dysfunctions
    crown chakra, 35
    heart chakra, 29
    root chakra, 23
    sacral plexus chakra, 25
    solar plexus chakra, 27
    third eye chakra, 33
    throat chakra, 31
physical chakras, 19
physical plane, safety and security
    in, 23
pineal gland, 33

pituitary gland, 35
pleasure, 24
pneumonia, 29
positive energy, maintaining, 48–49
power. *See also* solar plexus chakra
   chakra associated with, 19, 102
   and control, 25
   issues related to, 27
   prestige, need for, 26
   prostate cancer, 61
   purple, chakra associated with, 35

R

RA, chanting, 109
raised vibration, maintaining, 48–49
rectal tumors/cancer, 23, 61
red, association with root chakra, 23
red jasper, 23, 89
Reiki, 47
relationships
   dysfunctions, 62
   honor in, honor in, 25
   issues, 24
reproductive issues, 24
resentment, 29
ribs, 29
Roman chamomile essential oil,
   27, 107
root chakra. *See also* physical chakras
   adrenal fatigue, 56
   affirmation, 23
   anger, 56–57
   back pain, 60
   cancers, 61
   causes of energy blocks, 23
   chanting mantra, 93
   characteristics, 86
   codependency, 62
   color, 23
   constipation, 63–64
   crystals, 23, 89–90
   element, 23

essential oils, 23, 91
fear, 66–67
glands, 23
hemorrhoids, 69–70
infertility, 70–71
leg pain, 72
life lesson, 23
location, 23
meditations, 87–88
mental/emotional issues, 23
names, 23
in and out of harmony, 22
panic attacks, 74–75
physical body parts and
   dysfunctions, 23
purpose of, 19
Sanskrit name, 23
sciatica, 75–76
self-hate, 76
sexual abuse, 77
stress, 80–81
tips, 93
weight issues, 83
yoga, 92
rose essential oil, 29, 115
rose quartz, 29, 113
rosemary essential oil, 27, 31, 107, 123
rosewood essential oil, 25, 27, 99, 107
ruby, 23, 89
rutilated quartz, 27, 105

S

sacral plexus chakra
   affirmation, 25
   anger, 57
   back pain, 60
   cancers, 61
   causes of energy blocks, 25
   chanting mantra, 101
   characteristics, 94
   codependency, 62
   color, 25

conflict, 63
crystals, 25, 97–98
element, 25
essential oils, 25, 99
glands, 25
guilt, 68
hip pain, 70
infertility, 70–71
life lesson, 25
location, 25
meditations, 95–96
mental/emotional issues, 25
names, 25
in and out of harmony, 24
physical body parts and
    dysfunctions, 25
purpose of, 19
Sanskrit name, 25
sciatica, 75–76
sexual abuse, 77
shame, 78
STIs (sexually transmitted
    infections), 79
stress, 81
tips, 101
uterine fibroids and cysts, 82–83
weight issues, 83
yoga, 100
sacred healing space, creating, 50–51
safety and security issues, 23
sahasrara, 35
sandalwood essential oil, 23, 25, 33,
    35, 91, 99, 131, 139
Sanskrit names
    crown chakra, 35
    heart chakra, 29
    root chakra, 23
    sacral plexus chakra, 25
    solar plexus chakra, 27
    third eye chakra, 33
    throat chakra, 31

sciatica, 23, 75–76. See also back pain
scoliosis, 31
second chakra. See sacral plexus chakra
security, 86
seizures, 33
selenite, 35, 137
self-centeredness, 29
self-confidence, 27
self-empowerment, 27
self-esteem, 19, 26–27, 31, 102
self-expression, 30, 118
self-hate, 76. See also hatred and love
selflessness, 35
self-love, 28, 110
self-respect, 26–27
self-worth, 26
seventh chakra. See crown chakra
sexual abuse, 77
sexuality, 19, 23–25, 94
SHAM, chanting, 133
shame, 24, 78
shoulders, 29, 31
sinus pain, 78–79
sixth chakra. See third eye chakra
"sixth sense," 32
skeletal system, 35
skin issues, 35, 79–80
smoky quartz, 23, 89
smudging living spaces, 49, 89
sodalite, 31, 121
solar plexus chakra. See also power
    affirmation, 27
    anorexia, 57–58
    back pain, 60
    bulimia, 57–58
    cancers, 61
    causes of energy blocks, 27
    chanting mantra, 109
    characteristics, 102
    codependency, 62
    color, 27

conflict, 63
constipation, 63–64
crystals, 27, 105–106
digestive issues, 65
element, 27
essential oils, 27, 107
fatigue, 66
fear, 66–67
glands, 27
guilt, 68
infertility, 70–71
leg pain, 72
life lessons, 27
location, 27
meditations, 103–104
mental/emotional issues, 27
names, 27
in and out of harmony, 26
panic attacks, 74–75
physical body parts and
    dysfunctions, 27
purpose of, 19
Sanskrit names, 27
self-hate, 76
sexual abuse, 77
shame, 78
stomach pain/disorders, 80
stress, 81
tips, 109
weight issues, 83
yoga, 108
sound
    chakra associated with, 31
    sensitivity to, 35
Source, disconnection from, 34
spikenard, and root chakra, 23, 91
spinal difficulties, 33
spiritual chakras, identifying, 19
spirituality, chakra associated with,
    19, 35
spleen, 27

star sapphire, 33, 129
statues of deities, placing on altars, 51
stiff neck, 31
STIs (sexually transmitted
    infections), 79
stomach
    cancer, 61
    pain and disorders, 80
    and solar plexus chakra, 27
stress, 56, 80–81
stroke, 33
sugilite, 33, 129
sunstone, 25, 97
survival, chakra associated with, 19
svadisthana, 25
swollen glands, 31
symptoms and ailments, common,
    54–84

T
tanzanite, 33, 129
teeth and gums, 31
testicles, 25
third chakra. See solar plexus chakra
third eye chakra
    addiction, 55
    affirmation, 33
    causes of energy blocks, 33
    chanting mantra, 133
    characteristics, 126
    color, 33
    crystals, 33, 129–130
    element, 33
    essential oils, 33, 131
    glands, 33
    headaches, 68–69
    life lesson, 33
    location, 33
    meditations, 127–128
    mental/emotional issues, 33
    names, 33

neuropathy, 74
in and out of harmony, 32
physical body parts and
    dysfunctions, 33
purpose of, 19
Sanskrit name, 33
sinus pain, 78
stress, 81
tips, 133
yoga, 132
thought element, 35
throat chakra
addiction, 55
affirmation, 31
back pain, 60
cancers, 61
causes of energy blocks, 31
chanting mantra, 125
characteristics, 118
color, 31
conflict, 63
crystals, 31, 121–122
element, 31
essential oils, 31, 123
glands, 31
jaw pain, 71–72
life lesson, 31
location, 31
meditations, 119–120
mental/emotional issues, 31
names, 31
neck pain, 73–74
in and out of harmony, 30
physical body parts and
    dysfunctions, 31
purpose of, 19
Sanskrit name, 31
sexual abuse, 77
stress, 81
thyroid disorders, 82
tips, 125

TMJ (temporomandibular) pain,
    71–72
yoga, 124
thymus gland, 29
thyroid gland
cancer, 61
disorders, 82
and throat chakra, 31
TMJ (temporomandibular joint), 31,
    71–72
tolerance and acceptance, 26
trachea, 31
tribal consciousness, 22, 86
trust, 27, 29
truth, 31, 118
turquoise, 31, 121

U
ulcers, 27
Unity, living in knowledge of, 34
Universe, disconnection from, 34
upper back, chakras affected, 60
uterine fibroids and cysts, 82–83. See
    also womb

V
VAM, chanting, 101
varicose veins, 23
Vedas, 13
vetiver, and root chakra, 23, 91
vishuddha, 31
visualizations, practicing, 37–38

W
warrior fire, 102
weight issues, 23, 83
white, chakra associated with, 35
white sage, using, 49–50, 89
white topaz, 35, 137
womb, 25. See also uterine fibroids
    and cysts

Y

yellow, chakra associated
    with, 27
yellow agate, 27, 105
yellow citrine, 27, 105
yellow tiger's eye, 27, 105
yellow topaz, 27, 105
ylang ylang, 25, 29, 99, 115

yoga
    crown chakra, 140
    heart chakra, 116
    practicing, 41–43, 145
    root chakra, 92
    sacral plexus chakra, 100
    solar plexus chakra, 108
    third eye chakra, 132
    throat chakra, 124
YUM, chanting, 117

ACKNOWLEDGMENTS

• • • • • • •

I would like to express my gratitude to my patients and students, who allow me to assist them on their healing journeys, who open their hearts with deep courage, and who teach me something new about myself every day. Thanks to my family and ancestors for their support. Thanks to Jenn Lee Superstar and Jess Blake, who contributed their yoga expertise to this book. Thanks to Marc Gian for teaching me the wisdom of essential oil therapy as it relates to Traditional Chinese Medicine and the chakras. Thanks to Lauren Dobey for her guidance during the beginning phase of this book, and for cheering me on. Thanks to teachers Maria Socorro Laya-Smith and Barbara Fasulo who opened me to Reiki energy. Thanks to Kate Anjahlia Loye, who introduced me to my unique connection with Queen Cobra and Seshet, both of whose wisdom was instrumental in writing this manifestation. Gratitude to my partner, Stacey Alomar, for being a true source of support during the creation of this book, and for being grounded in his root chakra, on my behalf. Lastly, I am grateful to Spirit for waking me up, and the chakra system for being the amazing portal to our light.

ABOUT THE AUTHOR

• • • • • • •

Margarita Alcantara is a Licensed Acupuncturist, a Reiki Master and Teacher, and a natural empath. In her New York-based private practice, Alcantara Acupuncure, Margarita helps others reconnect to their inner light and Higher Selves—with knowledge, compassion, and fierce love—by sharing her own brand of powerful healing with them. In addition to Acupuncture and Reiki, Margarita has a rich knowledge base of multiple adjunctive acupuncture therapies and wellness disciplines, which she integrates into her patients' treatment as needed. She believes that physical healing is connected to spiritual and emotional healing, and provides guidance as her treatments activate the release of physical, spiritual, and emotional blockages.